MW01125260

The Story of Greeks

H A Guerber

Alpha Editions
New Delhi, India

DEDICATED

TO

ARNOLD, HELEN, and EDWARD

PREFACE.

This elementary history of Greece is intended for supplementary reading or as a first history text-book for young pupils. It is therefore made up principally of stories about persons; for, while history proper is largely beyond the comprehension of children, they are able at an early age to understand and enjoy anecdotes of people, especially of those in the childhood of civilization. At the same time, these stories will give a clear idea of the most important events that have taken place in the ancient world, and, it is hoped, will arouse a desire to read further. They also aim to enforce the lessons of perseverance, courage, patriotism, and virtue that are taught by the noble lives described.

A knowledge of ancient history, however superficial, is of very great value; and the classic legends are almost equally worth knowing, because of the prominent part they play in the world's literature. These tales make a deep impression on the minds of children, and the history thus learned almost in play will cling to the memory far more tenaciously than any lessons subsequently conned.

Many children leave school unacquainted with any history except that of the United States; which, dealing with less simple and primitive times than that of Greece, is apt to be so unattractive that the child never afterwards reads any historical works. It has been my intention to write a book which will give children pleasure to read, and will thus counteract the impression that history is uninteresting.

A few suggestions to teachers may not be considered superfluous. In the first place, I have found historical anecdotes an excellent aid in teaching English. Pupils find it far from irksome to relate the stories in their own words, and to reproduce them in compositions. Secondly, whenever a city or country is mentioned, every pupil should point out its location on the map. By such means only can any one properly understand an historical narrative; and in the present case there is the added reason that the practice will go far towards increasing the child's interest in geography. Lastly, the teacher should take great care that the proper names are correctly pronounced. The most common errors are provided against in the text; for, on the first occurrence of such a word, it is divided into syllables, with the accent marked. It remains for the teacher to enforce the ordinary rules as to the proper sounds of vowels and consonants.

H. A. G.

Theseus and the Minotaur.

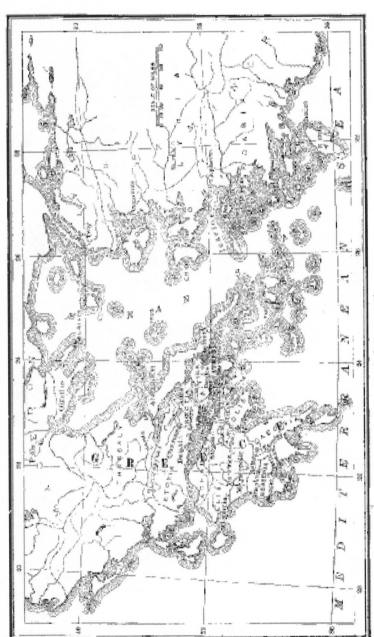

Map of Ancient Greece.

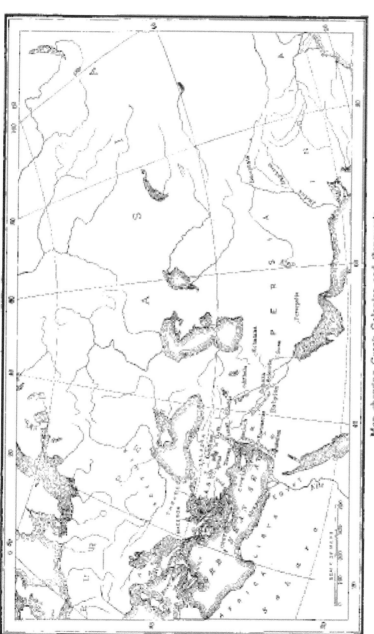

Map showing Greek Colonies and Conquests.

I. EARLY INHABITANTS OF GREECE.

Although Greece (or Hel'las) is only half as large as the State of New York, it holds a very important place in the history of the world. It is situated in the southern part of Europe, cut off from the rest of the continent by a chain of high mountains which form a great wall on the north. It is surrounded on nearly all sides by the blue waters of the Med-it-er-ra'ne-an Sea, which stretch so far inland that it is said no part of the country is forty miles from the sea, or ten miles from the hills. Thus shut in by sea and mountains, it forms a little territory by itself, and it was the home of a noted people.

The history of Greece goes back to the time when people did not know how to write, and kept no record of what was happening around them. For a long while the stories told by parents to their children were the only information which could be had about the country and its former inhabitants; and these stories, slightly changed by every new teller, grew more and more extraordinary as time passed. At last they were so changed that no one could tell where the truth ended and fancy began.

The beginning of Greek history is therefore like a fairy tale; and while much of it cannot, of course, be true, it is the only information we have about the early Greeks. It is these strange fireside stories, which used to amuse Greek children so many years ago, that you are first going to hear.

About two thousand years before the birth of Christ, in the days when Isaac wanted to go down into Egypt, Greece was inhabited by a savage race of men called the Pe-las'gi-ans. They lived in the forests, or in caves hollowed out of the mountain side, and hunted wild beasts with great clubs and stone-tipped arrows and spears. They were so rude and wild that they ate nothing but raw meat, berries, and the roots which they dug up with sharp stones or even with their hands.

For clothing, the Pelasgians used the skins of the beasts they had killed; and to protect themselves against other savages, they gathered together in families or tribes, each having a chief who led in war and in the chase.

There were other far more civilized nations in those days. Among these were the E-gyp'tians, who lived in Africa. They had long known the use of fire, had good tools, and were much further advanced than the Pelasgians. They had learned not only to build houses, but to erect the most wonderful monuments in the world,—the Pyr'a-mids, of which you have no doubt heard.

In Egypt there were at that time a number of learned men. They were acquainted with many of the arts and sciences, and recorded all they knew in a peculiar writing of their own invention. Their neighbors, the Phœ-ni'-cians, whose land also bordered on the Mediterranean Sea, were quite civilized too; and as both of these nations had ships, they soon began to sail all around that great inland sea.

As they had no compass, the Egyptian and Phœnician sailors did not venture out of sight of land. They first sailed along the shore, and then to the islands which they could see far out on the blue waters.

When they had come to one island, they could see another still farther on; for, as you will see on any map, the Mediterranean Sea, between Greece and Asia, is dotted with islands, which look like stepping-stones going from one coast to the other.

Advancing thus carefully, the Egyptians and Phœnicians finally came to Greece, where they made settlements, and began to teach the Pelasgians many useful and important things.

II. THE DELUGE OF OGYGES.

The first Egyptian who thus settled in Greece was a prince called In'a-chus. Landing in that country, which has a most delightful climate, he taught the Pelasgians how to make fire and how to cook their meat. He also showed them how to build comfortable homes by piling up stones one on top of another, much in the same way as the farmer makes the stone walls around his fields.

The Pelasgians were intelligent, although so uncivilized; and they soon learned to build these walls higher, in order to keep the wild beasts away from their homes. Then, when they had learned the use of bronze and iron tools, they cut the stones into huge blocks of regular shape.

These stone blocks were piled one upon another so cleverly that some of the walls are still standing, although no mortar was used to hold the stones together. Such was the strength of the Pelasgians, that they raised huge blocks to great heights, and made walls which their descendants declared must have been built by giants.

As the Greeks called their giants Cy'clops, which means "round-eyed," they soon called these walls Cy-clo-pe'an; and, in pointing them out to their children, they told strange tales of the great giants who had built them, and always added that these huge builders had but one eye, which was in the middle of the forehead.

Some time after Inachus the Egyptian had thus taught the Pelasgians the art of building, and had founded a city called Ar'gos, there came a terrible earthquake. The ground under the people's feet heaved and cracked, the mountains shook, the waters flooded the dry land, and the people fled in terror to the hills.

In spite of the speed with which they ran, the waters soon overtook them. Many of the Pelasgians were thus drowned, while their terrified companions ran faster and faster up the mountain, nor stopped to rest until they were quite safe.

Looking down upon the plains where they had once lived, they saw them all covered with water. They were now forced to build new homes; but when the waters little by little sank into the ground, or flowed back into the sea, they were very glad to find that some of their thickest walls had resisted the earthquake and flood, and were still standing firm.

The memory of the earthquake and flood was very clear, however. The poor Pelasgians could not forget their terror and the sudden death of so many friends, and they often talked about that horrible time. As this flood occurred in the days when Og'y-ges was king, it has generally been linked to his name, and called the Deluge (or flood) of Ogyges.

III. THE FOUNDING OF MANY IMPORTANT CITIES.

Some time after Inachus had built Argos, another Egyptian prince came to settle in Greece. His name was Ce'crops, and, as he came to Greece after the Deluge of Ogyges, he found very few inhabitants left. He landed, and decided to build a city on a promontory northeast of Argos. Then he invited all the Pelasgians who had not been drowned in the flood to join him.

The Pelasgians, glad to find such a wise leader, gathered around him, and they soon learned to plow the fields and to sow wheat. Under Cecrops' orders they also planted olive trees and vines, and learned how to press the oil from the olives and the wine from the grapes. Cecrops taught them how to harness their oxen; and before long the women began to spin the wool of their sheep, and to weave it into rough woolen garments, which were used for clothing, instead of the skins of wild beasts.

After building several small towns in At'ti-ca, Cecrops founded a larger one, which was at first called Ce-cro'pi-a in honor of himself. This name, however, was soon changed to Ath'ens to please A-the'ne (or Mi-ner'va), a goddess whom the people worshiped, and who was said to watch over the welfare of this her favorite city.

When Cecrops died, he was followed by other princes, who continued teaching the people many

Athene.

useful things, such as the training and harnessing of horses, the building of carts, and the proper way of harvesting grain. One prince even showed them how to make beehives, and how to use the honey as an article of food.

As the mountain sides in Greece are covered with a carpet of wild, sweet-smelling herbs and flowers, the Greekhoney is very good; and people say that the best honey in the world is made by the bees on Mount Hy-met'tus, near Athens, where they gather their golden store all summer long.

Shortly after the building of Athens, a Phœnician colony, led by Cad'mus, settled a neighboring part of the country, called Bœ-o'tia, where they founded the city which was later known as Thebes. Cadmus also taught the people many useful things, among others the art of trade (or commerce) and that of navigation (the building and using of ships); but, best of all, he brought the alphabet to Greece, and showed the people how to express their thoughts in writing.

Almost at the same time that Cadmus founded Thebes, an Egyptian called Dan'a-us came to Greece, and settled a colony on the same spot where that of Inachus had once been. The new Argos rose on the same place as the old; and the country around it, called Ar'go-lis, was separated from Bœotia and Attica only by a long narrow strip of land, which was known as the Isthmus of Cor'-inth.

Danaus not only showed the Pelasgians all the useful arts which Cadmus and Cecrops had taught, but also helped them to build ships like that in which he had come to Greece. He also founded religious festivals or games in honor of the harvest goddess, De-me'ter. The women were invited to these games, and they only were allowed to bear torches in the public processions, where they sang hymns in honor of the goddess.

The descendants of Danaus long ruled over the land; and one member of his family, Per'seus, built the town ofMy-ce'næ on a spot where many of the Pelasgian stone walls can still be seen.

The Pelasgians who joined this young hero helped him to build great walls all around his town. These were provided with massive gateways and tall towers, from which the soldiers could overlook the whole country, and see the approach of an enemy from afar.

The Lion Gate, Mycenæ.

This same people built tombs for some of the ancient kings, and many treasure and store houses. These buildings, buried under earth and rubbish, were uncovered a few years ago. In the tombs were found swords, spears, and remains of ancient armor, gold ornaments, ancient pieces of pottery, human bones, and, strangest of all, thin masks of pure gold, which covered the faces of some of the dead.

Thus you see, the Pelasgians little by little joined the new colonies which came to take possession of the land, and founded little states or countries of their own, each governed by its own king, and obeying its own laws.

IV. STORY OF DEUCALION.

The Greeks used to tell their children that Deu-ca´li-on, the leader of the Thes-sa´li-ans, was a descendant of the gods, for each part of the country claimed that its first great man was the son of a god. It was under the reign of Deucalion that another flood took place. This was even more terrible than that of Ogyges; and all the people of the neighborhood fled in haste to the high mountains north of Thes´sa-ly, where they were kindly received by Deucalion.

When all danger was over, and the waters began to recede, they followed their leader down into the plains again. This soon gave rise to a wonderful story, which you will often hear. It was said that Deucalion and his wife Pyr'rha were the only people left alive after the flood. When the waters had all gone, they went down the mountain, and found that the temple at Del'phi, where they worshiped their gods, was still standing unharmed. They entered, and, kneeling before the altar, prayed for help.

A mysterious voice then bade them go down the mountain, throwing their mother's bones behind them. They were very much troubled when they heard this, until Deucalion said that a voice from heaven could not have meant them to do any harm. In thinking over the real meaning of the words he had heard, he told his wife, that, as the Earth is the mother of all creatures, her bones must mean the stones.

Deucalion and Pyrrha, therefore, went slowly down the mountain, throwing the stones behind them. The Greeks used to tell that a sturdy race of men sprang up from the stones cast by Deucalion, while beautiful women came from those cast by Pyrrha.

The country was soon peopled by the children of these men, who always proudly declared that the story was true, and that they sprang from the race which owed its birth to this great miracle. Deucalion reigned over this people as long as he lived; and when he died, his two sons, Am-phic 'ty-on and Hel'len, became kings in his stead. The former staid in Thessaly; and, hearing that some barbarians called Thra'cians were about to come over the mountains and drive his people away, he called the chiefs of all the different states to a council, to ask their advice about the best means of defense. All the chiefs obeyed the summons, and met at a place in Thessaly where the mountains approach the sea so closely as to leave but a narrow pass between. In the pass are hot springs, and so it was called Ther-mop'y-læ, or the Hot Gateway.

The chiefs thus gathered together called this assembly the Am-phic-ty-on'ic Council, in honor of Amphictyon. After making plans to drive back the Thracians, they decided to meet once a year, either at Thermopylæ or at the temple at Delphi, to talk over all important matters.

V. STORY OF DÆDALUS AND ICARUS.

Hellen, Deucalion's second son, finding Thessaly too small to give homes to all the people, went southward with a band of hardy followers, and settled in another part of the country which we call Greece, but which was then, in honor of him, called Hellas, while his people were called Hel-le 'nes, or subjects of Hellen.

When Hellen died, he left his kingdom to his three sons, Do'rus, Æ'o-lus, and Xu'thus. Instead of dividing their father's lands fairly, the eldest two sons quarreled with the youngest, and finally drove him away. Homeless and poor, Xuthus now went to Athens, where he was warmly welcomed by the king, who not only treated him very kindly, but also gave him his daughter in marriage, and promised that he should inherit the throne.

This promise was duly kept, and Xuthus the exile ruled over Athens. When he died, he left the crown to his sons, I'on and A-chæ'us.

As the A-the'ni-ans had gradually increased in number until their territory was too small to afford a living to all the inhabitants, Ion and Achæus, even in their father's lifetime, led some of their followers along the Isthmus of Corinth, and down into the peninsula, where they founded two flourishing states, called, after them, A-cha'ia and I-o'ni-a. Thus, while northern Greece was pretty equally divided between the Do'ri-ans and Æ-o'li-ans, descendants and subjects of Dorus and Æolus, the peninsula was almost entirely in the hands of the I-o'ni-ans and A-chæ'ans, who built towns, cultivated the soil, and became bold navigators. They ventured farther and farther out at sea, until they were familiar with all the neighboring bays and islands.

Sailing thus from place to place, the Hellenes came at last to Crete, a large island south of Greece. This island was then governed by a very wise king called Mi'nos. The laws of this monarch were so just that all the Greeks admired them very much. When he died, they even declared that the gods had called him away to judge the dead in Ha´des, and to decide what punishments and rewards the spirits deserved.

Although Minos was very wise, he had a subject named Dæd´a-lus who was even wiser than he. This man not only invented the saw and the potter's wheel, but also taught the people how to rig sails for their vessels.

As nothing but oars and paddles had hitherto been used to propel ships, this last invention seemed very wonderful; and, to compliment Dædalus, the people declared that he had given their vessels wings, and had thus enabled them to fly over the seas.

Many years after, when sails were so common that they ceased to excite any wonder, the people, forgetting that these were the wings which Dædalus had made, invented a wonderful story, which runs as follows.

Minos, King of Crete, once sent for Dædalus, and bade him build a maze, or labyrinth, with so many rooms and winding halls, that no one, once in it, could ever find his way out again.

Dædalus set to work and built a maze so intricate that neither he nor his son Ic´a-rus, who was with him, could get out. Not willing to remain there a prisoner, Dædalus soon contrived a means of escape.

Dædalus and Icarus.

He and Icarus first gathered together a large quantity of feathers, out of which Dædalus cleverly made two pairs of wings. When these were fastened to their shoulders by means of wax, father and son rose up like birds and flew away. In spite of his father's cautions, Icarus rose higher and higher, until the heat of the sun melted the wax, so that his wings dropped off, and he fell into the sea and was drowned. His father, more prudent than he, flew low, and reached Greece in safety. There he went on inventing useful things, often gazing out sadly over the waters in which Icarus had perished, and which, in honor of the drowned youth, were long known as the I-ca´ri-an Sea.

VI. THE ADVENTURES OF JASON.

The Hellenes had not long been masters of all Greece, when a Phryg'i-an called Pe'lops became master of the peninsula, which from him received the name of Pel-o-pon-ne'sus. He first taught the people to coin money; and his descendants, the Pe-lop'i-dæ, took possession of all the land around them, with the exception of Argolis, where the Da-na'i-des continued to reign.

Some of the Ionians and Achæans, driven away from their homes by the Pelopidæ, went on board their many vessels, and sailed away. They formed Hel-len'ic colonies in the neighboring islands along the coast of Asia Minor, and even in the southern part of Italy.

As some parts of Greece were very thinly settled, and as the people clustered around the towns where their rulers dwelt, there were wide, desolate tracts of land between them. Here were many wild beasts and robbers, who lay in wait for travelers on their way from one settlement to another. The robbers, who hid in the forests or mountains, were generally feared and disliked, until at last some brave young warriors made up their minds to fight against them and to kill them all. These young men were so brave that they well deserved the name of heroes, which has always been given them; and they met with many adventures about which the people loved to hear. Long after they had gone, the inhabitants, remembering their relief when the robbers were killed, taught their children to honor these brave young men almost as much as the gods, and they called the time when they lived the Heroic Age.

Not satisfied with freeing their own country from wild men and beasts, the heroes wandered far away from home in search of further adventures. These have also been told over and over again to children of all countries and ages, until every one is expected to know something about them. Fifty of these heroes, for instance, went on board of a small vessel called the "Argo," sailed across the well-known waters, and ventured boldly into unknown seas. They were in search of a Golden Fleece, which they were told they would find in Col'chis, where it was said to be guarded by a great dragon.

The leader of these fifty adventurers was Ja'son, an Æolian prince, who brought them safely to Colchis, whence, as the old stories relate, they brought back the Golden Fleece. They also brought home the king's daughter, who married Jason, and ruled his kingdom with him. Of course, as there was no such thing as a Golden Fleece, the Greeks merely used this expression to tell about the wealth which they got in the East, and carried home with them; for the voyage of the "Argo" was in reality the first distant commercial journey undertaken by the Greeks.

VII. THESEUS VISITS THE LABYRINTH.

On coming back from the quest for the Golden Fleece, the heroes returned to their own homes, where they continued their efforts to make their people happy.

The'seus, one of the heroes, returned to Athens, and founded a yearly festival in honor of the goddess Athene. This festival was called Pan-ath-e-næ'a, which means "all the worshipers of Athene." It proved a great success, and was a bond of union among the people, who thus learned each other's customs and manners, and grew more friendly than if they had always staid at home. Theseus is one of the best-known among all the Greek heroes. Besides going with Jason in the "Argo," he rid his country of many robbers, and sailed to Crete. There he visited Minos, the king, who, having some time before conquered the Athenians, forced them to send him every year a shipload of youths and maidens, to feed to a monster which he kept in the Labyrinth.

To free his country from this tribute, Theseus, of his own free will, went on board the ship. When he reached Crete, he went first into the Labyrinth, and killed the monster with his sword. Then he found his way out of the maze by means of a long thread which the king's daughter had given him.

One end of it he carried with him as he entered, while the other end was fastened to the door.

His old father, Ӯgeus, who had allowed him to go only after much persuasion, had told him to change the black sails of his vessel for white if he were lucky enough to escape. Theseus promised to do so, but he entirely forgot it in the joy of his return.

Ægeus, watching for the vessel day after day, saw it coming back at last; and when the sunlight fell upon the black sails, he felt sure that his son was dead.

His grief was so great at this loss, that he fell from the rock where he was standing down into the sea, and was drowned. In memory of him, the body of water near the rock is still known as the Æge´an Sea.

When Theseus reached Athens, and heard of his father's grief and sudden death, his heart was filled with sorrow and remorse, and he loudly bewailed the carelessness which had cost his father's life.

Theseus now became King of Athens, and ruled his people very wisely for many years. He took part in many adventures and battles, lost two wives and a beloved son, and in his grief and old age became so cross and harsh that his people ceased to love him.

They finally grew so tired of his cruelty, that they all rose up against him, drove him out of the city, and forced him to take up his abode on the Island of Scy´ros. Then, fearing that he might return unexpectedly, they told the king of the island to watch him night and day, and to seize the first good opportunity to get rid of him. In obedience to these orders, the king escorted Theseus wherever he went; and one day, when they were both walking along the edge of a tall cliff, he suddenly pushed Theseus over it. Unable to defend or save himself, Theseus fell on some sharp rocks far below, and was instantly killed.

The Athenians rejoiced greatly when they heard of his death; but they soon forgot his harshness, remembered only his bravery and all the good he had done them in his youth, and regretted their ingratitude. Long after, as you will see, his body was carried to Athens, and buried not far from the A-crop´o-lis, which was a fortified hill or citadel in the midst of the city. Here the Athenians built a temple over his remains, and worshiped him as a god.

While Theseus was thus first fighting for his subjects, and then quarreling with them, one of his companions, the hero Her´cu-les (or Her´a-cles) went back to the Peloponnesus, where he had been born. There his descendants, the Her-a-cli´dæ, soon began fighting with the Pelopidæ for the possession of the land.

After much warfare, the Heraclidæ were driven away, and banished to Thessaly, where they were allowed to remain only upon condition that they would not attempt to renew their quarrel with the Pelopidæ for a hundred years.

VIII. THE TERRIBLE PROPHECY.

While Theseus was reigning over the Athenians, the neighboring throne of Thebes, in Bœotia, was occupied by King La´ius and Queen Jo-cas´ta. In those days the people thought they could learn about the future by consulting the oracles, or priests who dwelt in the temples, and pretended to give mortals messages from the gods.

Hoping to learn what would become of himself and of his family, Laius sent rich gifts to the temple at Delphi, asking what would befall him in the coming years. The messenger soon returned, but, instead of bringing cheerful news, he tremblingly repeated the oracle's words: "King Laius, you will have a son who will murder his father, marry his mother, and bring destruction upon his native city!"

This news filled the king's heart with horror; and when, a few months later, a son was born to him, he made up his mind to kill him rather than let him live to commit such fearful crimes. But Laius was too gentle to harm a babe, and so ordered a servant to carry the child out of the town and put him to death.

The man obeyed the first part of the king's orders; but when he had come to a lonely spot on the mountain, he could not make up his mind to kill the poor little babe. Thinking that the child would soon die if left on this lonely spot, the servant tied him to a tree, and, going back to the city, reported that he had gotten rid of him.

No further questions were asked, and all thought that the child was dead. It was not so, however. His cries had attracted the attention of a passing shepherd, who carried him home, and, being too poor to keep him, took him to the King of Corinth. As the king had no children, he gladly adopted the little boy.

When the queen saw that the child's ankles were swollen by the cord by which he had been hung to the tree, she tenderly cared for him, and called him Œd′i-pus, which means "the swollen-footed." This nickname clung to the boy, who grew up thinking that the King and Queen of Corinth were his real parents.

IX. THE SPHINX'S RIDDLE.

When Œdipus was grown up, he once went to a festival, where his proud manners so provoked one of his companions, that he taunted him with being only a foundling. Œdipus, seeing the frightened faces around him, now for the first time began to think that perhaps he had not been told the truth about his parentage. So he consulted an oracle.

Instead of giving him a plain answer,—a thing which the oracles were seldom known to do,—the voice said, "Œdipus, beware! You are doomed to kill your father, marry your mother, and bring destruction upon your native city!"

Horrified at this prophecy, and feeling sure that the King and Queen of Corinth were his parents, and that the oracle's predictions threatened misfortunes to them, Œdipus made up his mind to leave home forever. He did not even dare to return to bid his family good-by, and he started out alone and on foot to seek his fortunes elsewhere.

As he walked, he thought of his misfortunes, and grew very bitter against the cruel goddess of fate, whom he had been taught to fear. He fancied that this goddess could rule things as she pleased, and that it was she who had said he would commit the dreadful crimes which he was trying to avoid.

After several days' aimless wandering, Œdipus came at last to some crossroads. There he met an old man riding in a chariot, and preceded by a herald, who haughtily bade Œdipus make way for his master.

As Œdipus had been brought up as a prince, he was in the habit of seeing everybody make way for him. He therefore proudly refused to stir; and when the herald raised his staff to strike, Œdipus drew his sword and killed him.

The old man, indignant at this deed of violence, stepped out of his chariot and attacked Œdipus. Now, the young man did not know that it was his father Laius whom he thus met for the first time, so he fell upon and killed him also. The servants too were all slain when they in turn attacked him; and then Œdipus calmly continued his journey, little suspecting that the first part of the oracle's prediction had been fulfilled.

Soon after this fight, Œdipus came to the city of Thebes. The streets were filled with excited people, all talking at once; and the young prince, in listening to what they said, soon learned the cause of their excitement.

After a few moments' deep thought, Œdipus answered.

It seems that a terrible monster called the Sphinx had taken up its station on one of the principal roads leading to the town, and would allow no one to pass who could not answer a riddle which it asked. This creature had the head of a woman, the body of a lion, and the wings of an eagle; and, as it ate up all those who could not guess its riddle, the people were very much frightened.

Many persons had already been slain; for, although the bravest men had gone out to kill it, they had lost their lives in the attempt, as no one could harm it unless he guessed the mysterious riddle.

Laius, the king, hoping to learn from the oracle at Delphi the answer to the riddle, had ridden off in his chariot; but the people grew more excited still, when a messenger came running into the town, and said that the king and all his servants had been killed by robbers, and that their dead bodies had been found in the middle of the road.

Œdipus paid no attention to this news; for he little suspected that the old man whom he had killed was the king, whom everybody loved, and for whom they now mourned with noisy grief.

He was, however, deeply interested in the story of the Sphinx; and he was so sure that he could guess the riddle, that he immediately set out to find the monster. He walked boldly along the road until stopped by the Sphinx, which told him to answer this riddle if he wished to live: "What creature walks upon four feet in the morning, upon two at noon, and upon three at night?"

After a few moments' deep thought, Œdipus answered that the creature was *man*. "For," said he, "in the morning of life, or in babyhood, man creeps on hands and knees; at noon, or in manhood, he walks erect; and at evening, or in old age, he supports his tottering steps with a staff."

The Sphinx's riddle was guessed; and the monster, knowing that its power was now at an end, tried to get away. But Œdipus would not allow it to do so; and, drawing his sword, he forced it back until it fell over a precipice, on the sharp stones below, and was dashed to pieces.

X. BLINDNESS AND DEATH OF ŒDIPUS.

Bœotia was now rid of the Sphinx; and when the The´bans heard the joyful news of its death, they welcomed [Oe]dipus with much joy. In reward for his bravery, they gave him not only the throne, but also the hand of Jocasta, the widowed queen. It was thus that Œdipus, although he did not know it, fulfilled the second part of the prophecy, and married his own mother.

Several years now passed by, during which Œdipus ruled the Thebans so wisely, that they all loved him dearly, and went to him for advice in all their troubles. Finally the good times came to an end; and the people were again terrified, because a plague, or great sickness, broke out in the city, and many of the inhabitants died.

All kinds of medicines were tried, but without effect; and all the gods were asked to lend their aid. In despair, Œdipus sent a messenger to Delphi to ask the oracle how the disease could be stopped. The oracle for once gave a plain answer, and said that the plague would cease only when the murderer of Laius had been found and punished.

Investigations were now made for the first time, and it was found that Œdipus was the one who had slain the king. At the same time, the servant confessed that he had not killed the royal child; and the shepherd told how he had found the babe and carried him to Corinth, where he had been adopted by the king.

When Œdipus heard all this, he was driven almost mad with despair; for now he knew not only that he had murdered his father and married his mother, but that it was on his account that the plague had caused the death of so many people in Thebes.

In her horror and grief at this discovery, Queen Jocasta killed herself. When Œdipus learned that she was dead, he ran into the room where she lay, and took one of the buckles which fastened her dress and put out his eyes with it, saying, that, since they had beheld such a sorrowful sight, they should never again see the light of day.

To rid the city of his accursed presence, and thus, if possible, save it from the threatened destruction, Œdipus banished himself, and wandered away, old, blind, and poor, for he would take none of his riches with him.

He departed sorrowfully, leaving his kingdom to his two sons, E-te´o-cles and Pol-y-ni´ces, and telling them to care for their sisters, An-tig´o-ne and Is-me´ne.

Ismene wept bitterly when she said good-by to her father; but Antigone placed her father's hand upon her shoulder, said that she would never forsake him, and left the city, tenderly supporting and guiding him.

Father and daughter wandered thus from place to place, finding no rest; for all the people shrank from even looking upon Œdipus, who, they said, was evidently accursed by the gods, since he had committed such frightful crimes.

After many days' wandering and much fatigue, the exiles arrived at last on the border of a dark forest held sacred to the Furies,—the goddesses whose duty it was to punish all criminals by tormenting them as long as they lived, and even after they had died.

When Antigone described to her poor blind father the place they had reached, he bade her remain by the roadside, and, groping his way, soon vanished into the forest. He had scarcely gone, when a terrible thunderstorm arose. The air grew dark, the lightning flashed, the thunder rolled, the trees bent and twisted in the wind; and, although Antigone called her father again and again, she heard no answering cry.

When morning came, she went to look for him, but found no trace of him. The people in the neighborhood then told her that the Furies had dragged her father away to punish him for his crimes, and Antigone sadly went back to Thebes.

As soon as she arrived in the city, Antigone hastened to the palace to tell her brothers and sister about their father's sad death; but when she entered her former happy home, she learned that there are sadder things than death, for her brothers were no longer friends, and had begun a terrible quarrel.

XI. THE BROTHERS' QUARREL.

The misfortunes of Thebes had not come to an end with the banishment of Œdipus, and fate was still against the unhappy city. The plague, it is true, had stopped; but the two young princes were quarreling about the possession of the throne.

Both wanted to reign, and neither wished to share the throne with his brother. After much dispute, they agreed at last that each should reign a year in turn.

Eteocles, the elder, was of course allowed to rule during the first year; while Polynices went to pay a visit to A-dras'tus, King of Argos. Here he was warmly welcomed and hospitably entertained; but when the year was ended, he hurried back to Thebes to reign in his turn.

When he came to the city, however, Eteocles refused to give up the scepter, and, calling out his guards, made use of his power to drive Polynices out of the town. This was very wrong, for a promise should always be kept; and it made Polynices so angry, that he said he would return with an army, and force his brother to act fairly.

Polynices therefore hurried back to Argos, and soon persuaded Adrastus, with five other kings and noted warriors, to go with him to Thebes, and help him take the throne by force.

When Eteocles heard that seven kings were coming with a large army to make him give up the throne of Thebes, he made up his mind to fight hard to keep it. After strengthening the city walls, laying in a great stock of provisions, and securing the help of seven brave allies, Eteocles closed the gates of Thebes, and calmly awaited the arrival of the enemy.

Meanwhile the seven chiefs were marching from Argos to Thebes. They came at last to the forest of Ne'me-a, where Hercules, the chief hero of Argos, had once slain a terrible lion. This monster had long lived in the forest, filling the hearts of all the people with dread; and when Hercules came out of the forest, wearing the skin of the lion, they had greatly rejoiced.

Hercules and the Nemean Lion.

In honor of Hercules' victory over the Ne'me-an lion, the seven chiefs stopped in this spot to celebrate games, which they said should be held in that neighborhood every three years. This festival was ever after celebrated thus; and when the people gathered together there to see the racing and boxing, they loved to recall the memory of the brave lion slayer, and of the seven kings who had first celebrated the Nemean games.

When Polynices and his allies came at last to Thebes, they found all the gates closed; and although they fought bravely, and tried hard to enter the city, they were kept at bay for seven long years. At the end of that time the people inside the city, and those without, were equally tired of this long siege: so it was finally agreed that the two armies should meet on a neighboring plain and fight it out.

The armies were led by the two brothers, who now hated each other so bitterly, that, instead of waiting for the signal for battle, they rushed upon each other, and both fell before any one could interfere.

This terrible end of their quarrel filled the hearts of both armies with fear, and they agreed to make a truce in order to bury their chiefs. As it was customary at that time to burn the bodies of the dead, both corpses were laid upon the funeral pyre side by side. When the wood was all burned, the ashes were put into separate urns, for the Greeks used to tell their children that these brothers hated each other so much that even their ashes would not mingle.

This story of Œdipus and his family is only a myth, but it is a very celebrated one. The Greeks wrote stories, poems, and plays about it, and it is on that account that it should be known by every one who wishes to study the history of Greece.

XII. THE TAKING OF THEBES.

The terrible death of the two brothers Eteocles and Polynices did not, as you might suppose, end the siege of Thebes. No sooner were their funerals over, than both armies began to fight again; and they continued the contest until all the chiefs had been killed except Adrastus only.

Most of the soldiers had also been slain: so Adrastus made up his mind to go home, and wait until the sons of these fallen heroes were old enough to fight, before he went on with the war. As they thought it their duty to avenge all injuries, and especially the death of a relative, Adrastus had no trouble in getting these youths to march against Thebes. So they began a second siege, which was known as the War of the E-pig´o-ni, or descendants, because the young warriors took up their fathers' quarrel.

Such was the bravery of these young men, that they succeeded where their fathers had failed, and after a long struggle took the city of Thebes. As Polynices was dead, and could not claim the scepter he had so longed to possess, they put his son Ther-san´der upon the throne.

This young man ruled for a while in peace; but because his sons were insane, the Thebans thought that the gods still hated the race of Œdipus: so they drove these princes away, and chose another and less unlucky family to rule over them instead.

Even the daughters of Œdipus were very unhappy; for Antigone, having taken the part of her brother Polynices, was put to death, while her sister Ismene died of grief.

Such was the end of the race of Œdipus,—a king who has been considered the most unhappy man that ever lived, because, although he meant to be good, he was forced by fate to commit the most horrible crimes.

XIII. THE CHILDHOOD OF PARIS.

In those days, Pri´am and Hec´u-ba were King and Queen of Troy (or Il´i-um),—a beautiful city near the coast of Asia Minor, almost opposite Athens. They were the parents of a large family of sons and daughters; and among the sons were Hec´tor and Par´is, young men of remarkable strength and beauty.

Paris had had a very adventurous life. When he was but a little babe, his mother dreamed that she saw a flaming brand in the cradle, in the place where the child lay. This brand seemed to set fire to the cradle and all the palace; and the queen, awaking with a start, was overjoyed to find that it was nothing but a dream.

Men in those days believed that dreams were sent by the gods to warn them of coming events, and so Hecuba was very anxious to know what the burning brand meant. She told her husband all about it, and they finally decided to ask an oracle to explain the dream.

A few days later the messenger they had sent to the oracle came home, and Hecuba shed many tears when he brought word that the child Paris was destined to bring destruction upon his native city.

To escape this calamity, Priam ordered that Paris should be carried out of the city, and that he should be left in a forest, where the wild beasts would eat him up, or where he would be sure to die from hunger and cold.

Poor little Paris was therefore lifted out of his comfortable cradle, and left alone in the woods, where he cried so hard that a passing hunter heard him. This man was so sorry for the poor child, that he carried him home to his wife, who brought the little stranger up with her own children.

As he lived with hunters, Paris soon learned their ways; and he became so active that when he was quite grown up he went to Troy to take part in the athletic games, which were often held there in honor of the gods. He was so strong that he easily won all the prizes, although Hector and the other young princes were also striving for them.

When Paris went up to receive the crown of wild olive leaves which was the victor's prize, every one noticed his likeness to the royal family; and his sister Cas-san'dra, who was able to foretell future events, said that he was the son of Priam and Hecuba, and that he would bring great misfortunes upon Troy.

The king and queen paid no heed to these words, but gladly welcomed Paris home, and lavished all kinds of gifts upon him to make up for their cruelty and long neglect.

Paris was so fond of change and adventure, that he soon grew tired of court life, and asked Priam for a ship, so that he might sail off to Greece.

This request was readily granted, and Paris went away. The young prince sailed from island to island, and came at last to the southern part of the Peloponnesus, where the descendants of Hercules had founded the city of Sparta. Here he was warmly welcomed by King Men-e-la'us; but this king was obliged to leave home shortly after the arrival of Paris, and he bade Helen, his wife, the most beautiful woman in the world, do all she could to entertain the noble stranger.

Helen was so kind to Paris that he soon fell in love with her. His greatest wish was to have her as his wife: so he began to tell her that Ve'nus, the goddess of love, had promised him that he should marry the most beautiful woman in the world.

Talking thus day after day, the handsome young Paris finally persuaded Helen to leave her husband and home. She got on board of his vessel, and went with him to Troy as his wife. Of course, this wrongdoing could not bring happiness; and not only were they duly punished, but, as you will soon see, the crime of Paris brought suffering and death to his friends as well.

Menelaus.

When Menelaus came home and found that his guest had run away with his wife, he was very angry, and vowed that he would not rest until he had punished Paris and won back the beautiful

Helen.

He therefore made ready for war, and sent word to his friends and relatives to come and help him, telling them to meet him at Au´lis, a seaport, where they would find swift-sailing vessels to carry them across the sea to Troy.

XIV. THE MUSTER OF THE TROOPS.

When the neighboring kings and chiefs received Menelaus' message, they were delighted; for fighting was their only occupation, and they enjoyed the din of battle more than anything else. They began to collect their soldiers, polish their arms, and man their vessels. Then, inviting all who wished to join them, they started out for Aulis, where they formed a huge army.

Each of the parties was led by its own king or chief. Some of these chiefs were very brave, and their names are still well known. The leading ones among them were Nes´tor, the wisest man of his day, to whom every one came for good advice; and U-lys´ses, the crafty or sly king, who was so clever that he could easily outwit all men.

There were also A´jax, the strongest man of his time; Thersander, the new king of Thebes, who came with the Epigoni; and Ag-a-mem´non, King of Mycenæ, Menelaus' brother, who was chosen chief of the whole army.

The Greeks never began any undertaking without consulting the oracles to find out how it would end. Agamemnon, therefore, consulted one of these soothsayers, who said that Troy would never be taken unless A-chil´les fought with the Greeks.

When they heard this answer, the chiefs immediately asked who Achilles was, and they soon learned all about him. He was a young prince of whom it had been foretold at the time of his birth that he would be the greatest warrior of his age, and that he would die young. His mother, who loved him dearly, shed many tears when she heard these words, and made up her mind to do all she could to prevent this prophecy from coming true.

She first carried Achilles, when but a baby, to the river Styx, for it was said that those who bathed in its waters could never be wounded.

Afraid to let go of her child for fear he might drown, but anxious to make sure that the waters should touch every part of him, the mother plunged him into the rushing tide, holding him fast by one heel.

This she held so tight that the waters never even wet it; and it was only long after, when too late to remedy it, that an oracle told her that Achilles could be wounded in his heel, which the waters of the Styx had not touched. As soon as this good mother heard the first news of the coming war, her heart was troubled; for she knew that Achilles, who was now a young man, would want to join the army, and she was afraid of losing him.

To prevent his hearing anything about the war, she persuaded him to visit the King of Scyros. There, under pretext of a joke, he was induced to put on girl's clothes, and to pretend that he was a woman.

The Greeks, after hearing the oracle's words, sent messengers for Achilles; but they could not find him, as he had left home, and no one would tell them where he had gone. As it was of no use to set out without him, according to the oracle's answer, which they thoroughly believed, the army lingered at Aulis in despair.

Ulysses, seeing that they would never start unless Achilles were found, now offered to go and get him. Disguised as a peddler, with a pack upon his back, he went first to Achilles' home, where the chattering maids told him all he wished to know, and thence he went to the Island of Scyros.

Achilles was so well disguised that Ulysses could not tell him from the king's daughters and their maids: so he made use of a trick to find him out. Among the trinkets in his pack, he put a sword of fine workmanship, and, entering the palace, spread out his wares before the admiring maidens. They all gathered about him; but, while the real girls went into raptures over his ornaments, Achilles grasped the sword, drew it from the scabbard, carefully tested the blade, and swung it with a strong arm.

Of course, Ulysses then easily saw that he was not a girl, and, slipping up to him, managed to whisper news of the coming war, and won his promise to join the army at Aulis in a few days.

XV. THE SACRIFICE OF IPHIGENIA.

True to his promise, Achilles soon came to Aulis with his well-trained soldiers, the Myr'mi-dons, and with him came his friend Pa-tro'clus. All were now eager to start, and ready to embark; but unfortunately there was no favorable wind to fill their sails and waft them over to Asia Minor.

Day after day they waited, and offered sacrifices to the gods, but all in vain. At last they again consultedthe oracle, who said that the wind would not blow until Iph-i-ge-ni'a, Agamemnon's daughter, were offered up in sacrifice to Di-an'a, goddess of the moon and the chase, whom this king had once offended.

Agamemnon at first said that he would not sacrifice his daughter, but finally his companions persuaded him to do so. Just as the priest was about to kill the maiden on the altar, however, the goddess Diana came, and carried her off unharmed, leaving a deer to be sacrificed in her stead.

The deer was killed, the wind rose, the sails filled, and the Greek fleet soon came within sight of the high walls and towers of Troy. There, contrary to their expectations, the Greeks found the people ready to fight them; but, after many days' struggle, they saw that they had made no great advance.

On the wide plain which stretched out between the city and the sea, the Greek and Tro'jan armies fought many a battle; and sometimes one party, and sometimes the other, had the victory. The men on both sides had been trained to handle their weapons with great skill, and there were many fights in which the Greek heroes met the bravest Trojans.

Nine years passed thus in continual warfare, but even then the Greeks were as far from taking the town as on the first day; and the Trojans, in spite of all their courage, had not been able to drive their enemies away.

XVI. THE WRATH OF ACHILLES.

In all their battles, the booty won by the Greeks from the enemy had been divided among the chiefs and soldiers, and on one occasion female slaves were given to Agamemnon and Achilles. These girls were not born slaves, but were captives of war reduced to slavery, as was then the custom; for, while the men and boys were always killed, the women and girls were forced to be the servants of the victors.

Now, it happened that the slave given to Agamemnon was the daughter of a priest of A-pol´lo. He was very sorry when he heard she had fallen into the hands of the Greeks, and sent a message to Agamemnon, offering to give him a large sum of money if he would only set her free.

Agamemnon would not accept the money, and sent a rude message to the priest, who, in anger, asked Apollo to avenge this insult by sending a plague upon the Greeks. The god heard and granted this prayer, and soon all the soldiers in the Greek camp were suffering from a terrible disease, of which many of them died.

As no remedy could relieve the sufferers, the Greek leaders consulted an oracle, to find out how the plague might be stopped. Then they learned that Apollo was angry with Agamemnon because he had refused to give up his slave, and that the Greeks would continue to suffer until he made up his mind to give her back to her father.

Thus forced to give her up to save his men from further suffering and even from death, Agamemnon angrily said he would take Achilles' slave instead, and he had her brought to wait upon him in his tent.

Achilles, who wanted to save the Greeks from the plague, allowed the maiden to depart, warning Agamemnon, however, that he would no longer fight for a chief who could be so selfish and unjust. As soon as the girl had gone, therefore, he laid aside his fine armor; and although he heard the call for battle, and the din of fighting, he staid quietly within his tent.

While Achilles sat thus sulking day after day, his companions were bravely fighting. In spite of their bravery, however, the Trojans were gaining the advantage; for, now that Achilles was no longer there to fill their hearts with terror, they fought with new courage.

The Greeks, missing the bright young leader who always led them into the midst of the fray, were gradually driven back by the Trojans, who pressed eagerly forward, and even began to set fire to some of the Greek ships.

Achilles' friend, Patroclus, who was fighting at the head of the Greeks, now saw that the Trojans, unless they were checked, would soon destroy the whole army, and he rushed into Achilles' tent to beg him to come and help them once more.

His entreaties were vain. Achilles refused to move a step; but he consented at last to let Patroclus wear his armor, and, thus disguised, make a last attempt to rally the Greeks and drive back the Trojans.

Patroclus started out, and, when the Trojans saw the well-known armor, they shrank back in terror, for they greatly feared Achilles. They soon saw their mistake, however; and Hector, rushing forward, killed Patroclus, tore the armor off his body, and retired to put it on in honor of his victory.

Then a terrible struggle took place between the Trojans and the Greeks for the possession of Patroclus' body. The news of his friend's death had quickly been carried to Achilles, and had roused him from his indifferent state. Springing upon the wall that stretched before the camp, he gave a mighty shout, at the sound of which the Trojans fled, while Ajax and Ulysses brought back the body of Patroclus.

XVII. DEATH OF HECTOR AND ACHILLES.

The next day, having secured armor and weapons, Achilles again went out to fight. His purpose was to meet Hector, and, by killing him, to avenge his dead friend, Patroclus. He therefore rushed up and down the battlefield; and when at last he came face to face with his foe, they closed in deadly fight. The two young men, each the champion warrior of his army, were now fighting with the courage of despair; for, while Achilles was thirsting to avenge his friend, Hector knew that the fate of Troy depended mostly upon his arm. The struggle was terrible. It was watched with breathless interest by the armies on both sides, and by aged Priam and the Trojan women from the walls of Troy. In spite of Hector's courage, in spite of all his skill, he was doomed to die, and soon he fell under the blows of Achilles.

Then, in sight of both armies and of Hector's weeping family, Achilles took off his enemy's armor, bound the dead body by the feet to his chariot, and dragged it three times around the city walls before he went back to camp to mourn over the remains of Patroclus.

That night, guided by one of the gods, old King Priam came secretly into the Greek camp, and, stealing into Achilles' tent, fell at his feet. He had come to beg Achilles to give back the body of Hector, that he might weep over it, and bury it with all the usual ceremonies and honors.

Touched by the old man's tears, and ready now to listen to his better feelings, Achilles kindly raised the old king, comforted him with gentle words, and not only gave back the body, but also promised that there should be a truce of a few days, so that both armies could bury their dead in peace.

The funerals were held, the bodies burned, the usual games celebrated; and when the truce was over, the long war was begun again. After several other great fights, Achilles died from a wound in his heel caused by a poisoned arrow that was treacherously shot by Paris.

The sorrowing Greeks then buried the young hero on the wide plain between Troy and the sea. This spot has been visited by many people who admired the brave young hero of the Il´i-ad (see p. 60).

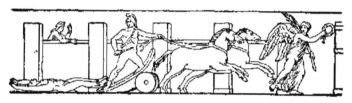

XVIII. THE BURNING OF TROY.

As the valor of the Greeks had proved of no avail during the ten-years' war, and as they were still as far as ever from taking Troy, Ulysses the crafty now proposed to take the city by a stratagem, or trick.

The Greeks, obeying his directions, built a wooden horse of very large size. It was hollow, and the space inside it was large enough to hold a number of armed men. When this horse was finished, and the men were hidden in it, the Greeks all embarked as if to sail home.

The Trojans, who had watched them embark and sail out of sight, rushed down to the shore shouting for joy, and began to wander around the deserted camp. They soon found the huge wooden horse, and were staring wonderingly at it, when they were joined by a Greek who had purposely been left behind, and who now crept out of his hiding place.

In answer to their questions, this man said that his companions had deserted him, and that the wooden horse had been built and left there as an offering to Po-sei´don (or Nep´tune), god of the sea. The Trojans, believing all this, now decided to keep the wooden horse in memory of their long siege, and the useless attempt of the Greeks to take Troy.

They therefore joyfully dragged the huge animal into the city; and, as the gates were not large enough for it to pass through, they tore down part of their strong walls.

That very night, while all the Trojans were sleeping peacefully for the first time in many years, without any fear of a midnight attack, the Greek vessels noiselessly sailed back to their old moorings. The soldiers landed in silence, and, marching up softly, joined their companions, who had crept out of the wooden horse, and had opened all the gates to receive them.

Pouring into Troy on all sides at once, the Greeks now began their work of destruction, killing, burning, and stealing everywhere. The Trojan warriors, awakening from sleep, vainly tried to defend themselves; but all were killed except Prince Æ-ne´as, who escaped with his family and a few faithful friends, to form a new kingdom in Italy.

All the women, including even the queen and her daughters, were made prisoners and carried away by the Greek heroes. The men were now very anxious to return home with the booty they had won; for they had done what they had long wished to do, and Troy, the beautiful city, was burned to the ground.

Vase.

All this, as you know, happened many years ago,—so many that no one knows just how long. The city thus destroyed was never rebuilt. Some years ago a German traveler began to dig on the spot where it once stood. Deep down under the ground he found the remains of beautiful buildings, some pottery, household utensils, weapons, and a great deal of gold, silver, brass, and bronze. All these things were blackened or partly melted by fire, showing that the Greeks had set fire to the city, as their famous old poems relate.

The Greeks said, however, that their gods were very angry with many of their warriors on account of the cruelty they showed on that dreadful night, and that many of them had to suffer great hardships before they reached home. Some were tossed about by the winds and waves for many long years, and suffered shipwrecks. Others reached home safely, only to be murdered by relatives who had taken possession of their thrones during their long absence.

Jug.

Only a few among these heroes escaped with their lives, and wandered off to other countries to found new cities. Thus arose many Greek colonies in Sicily and southern Italy, which were called Great Greece, in honor of the country from which the first settlers had come.

As you have already seen, Prince Æneas was among these Trojans. After many exciting adventures, which you will be able to read in the "Story of Rome," he sailed up the Ti´ber River, and landed near the place where one of his descendants was to found the present capital of Italy, which is one of the most famous cities in the world.

Cup.

XIX. HEROIC DEATH OF CODRUS.

You remember, do you not, how the sons of Pelops had driven the Heraclidæ, or sons of Hercules, out of the peninsula which was called the Peloponnesus? This same peninsula is now called Mo-re ´a, or the mulberry leaf, because it is shaped something like such a leaf, as you will see by looking at your map.

The Heraclidæ had not gone away willingly, but were staying in Thessaly, in the northern part of Greece, where they promised to remain one hundred years without making any attempt to come back.

Shortly after the end of the Trojan War, this truce of a hundred years came to an end; and the Heraclidæ called upon their neighbors the Dorians to join them, and help them win back their former lands.

Led by three brave chiefs, the allies passed through Greece proper, along the Isthmus of Corinth, and, spreading all over the Peloponnesus, soon took possession of the principal towns. The leading members of the family of Hercules took the title of kings, and ruled over the cities of Argos, Mycenæ, and Spar´ta.

The Dorians, who had helped the Heraclidæ win back their former possessions, now saw that the land here was better than their home in the mountains, so they drove all the rest of the Ionians out of the country, and settled there also.

Thus driven away by the Dorians and the Heraclidæ, these Ionians went to Athens, to the neighboring islands, and even to the coast of Asia Minor, south of the ruined city of Troy, where they settled in great numbers. They called the strip of land which they occupied Ionia, and founded many towns, some of which, such as Eph´e-sus and Mi-le´tus, were destined to become famous.

Of course, the Ionians were very angry at thus being driven away from home; and those who had gone to live in Athens soon asked Co´drus, the Athenian king, to make war against the Heraclidæ of Sparta.

The two armies soon met, and prepared for battle. Codrus, having consulted an oracle, had learned that the victory would be given to the army whose king should be killed, so he nobly made up his mind to die for the good of his people.

Instead of going into battle in royal dress, with his guards all around him, as was his habit, he dressed himself like an ordinary soldier, and went forward until he stood in the very first rank of the army. Then he rushed boldly into the midst of the foe.

Of course, he was soon cut down; but the Athenians, seeing his courage, and learning why he had thus risked his life, fought with such valor that they defeated the Spar´tan forces, and forced them to retreat.

The victory had been won; but the Athenians were so sorry to lose their beloved king, that they could not rejoice, and sadly returned home, carrying the body of Codrus. Such was the admiration of all the people for this act of royal courage, that they vowed they would never again call any one by the name of king.

When Codrus had been buried, therefore, the Athenians gave his son and heir the government of the city, calling him archon, or chief for life,—a title which was borne by many rulers after him.

The Spartans, who had come into Attica to fight the Athenians, retreated hastily after their defeat, and returned to their city, where they settled, forcing all the people who dwelt in the neighborhood either to leave the country or to serve them as their slaves.

The return of the Heraclidæ into the Peloponnesus is the last event of the Heroic Age, and now real history begins. After this, it is no longer necessary to try to find out the truth hidden in the old tales which were handed down from father to son, and which were the only fairy stories the Greek children knew; for henceforth records were kept of all the principal events.

XX. THE BLIND POET.

Homer.

Three or four centuries after the siege of Troy, there lived a poor old blind poet who wandered about from place to place, playing upon his lyre, and reciting wonderful verses which told about the adventures of the Greek heroes, and their great deeds during the Trojan War.

We are told that this old man, whose name was Ho´mer, had not always been poor and blind, but that, having embarked by mistake upon a vessel manned by pirates, he not only had been robbed of all his wealth, and blinded, but had been left upon a lonely shore.

By some happy chance, poor blind Homer found his way to the inhabited parts of the country, where he soon won many friends. Instead of spending all his time in weeping over his troubles, Homer tried to think of some way in which he could earn his living, and at the same time give pleasure to others. He soon found such a way in telling the stories of the past to all who cared to listen to them.

As the people in those days had no books, no schools, and no theaters, these stories seemed very wonderful. Little by little Homer turned them into verses so grand and beautiful that we admire them still; and these he recited, accompanying himself on a lyre, which he handled with much skill. As he wandered thus from place to place, old and young crowded around him to listen to his tales; and some young men were so struck by them that they followed him everywhere, until they too could repeat them. This was quite easy to do, because Homer had put them into the most beautiful and harmonious language the world has ever known. As soon as these young men had learned a few of the tales, they too began to travel from place to place, telling them to all they met; and thus Homer's verses became well known throughout all Greece.

Telling Homer's Tales.

The Greeks who could recite Homer's poems went next to the islands and Asia Minor, stopping at every place where Greek was spoken, to tell about the wrath of Achilles, the death of Patroclus, Hector, or old Priam, the burning of Troy, the wanderings of Ulysses, and the return of the Greeks. Other youths learned the poems; and so, although they were not written down for many a year, they were constantly recited and sung, and thus kept alive in the memory of the people.

As for Homer, their author, we know but little about him. We are told that he lived to be very old, and that although he was poor as long as he lived, and forced to earn his living by reciting his songs, he was greatly honored after his death.

His two great heroic poems—the Iliad, telling all about the Trojan War, and the Od´ys-sey, relating how Ulysses sailed about for ten years on his way home from Troy—were finally written down, and kept so carefully that they can still be read to-day. Such was the admiration felt for these poems, that some years after Homer's death an attempt was made to find out more about him, and about the place where he was born.

Fifty cities claimed the honor of giving him birth; but, although it was never positively found out where he was born, most people thought the Island of Chi´os was his birthplace. The Greek towns, wishing to show how much they admired the works of Homer, used to send yearly gifts to this place, the native land of the grandest poet the world has ever known.

XXI. THE RISE OF SPARTA.

The city of Sparta, founded in the days of the Pelasgians, and once ruled over by Menelaus and Helen, had fallen, as we have seen, into the hands of the Heraclidæ when they came back to the Peloponnesus after their exile of a hundred years. It was first governed by A-ris-to-de´mus, one of their three leaders; and, as records soon began to be kept, we know a great deal about the early history of this famous place.

As the town had formerly belonged to the Heraclidæ, and had been ruled by one of their ancestors, called Lac-e-dæ´mon, they called it by his name, and the country around it they named La-co´ni-a. Having won back the town by fighting, the Heraclidæ said that they would attend to war and politics, and make the conquered people till the ground.

The old inhabitants of Laconia, therefore, went on living in the country, where they sowed and harvested for the benefit of the Spartans. All the prisoners of war, however, became real slaves. They were obliged to serve the Spartans in every way, and were called He´lots.

When Aristodemus died, his twin sons were both made kings; and, as each of them left his throne to his descendants, Sparta had two kings, instead of one, from this time on. One member of the royal family, although he never bore the name of king, is the most noted man in Spartan history. This is Ly-cur´gus, the son of one ruler, the brother of another, and the guardian of an infant king named Char-i-la´us.

Lycurgus was a thoroughly good and upright man. We are told that the mother of the baby king once offered to put her child to death that Lycurgus might reign. Fearing for the babe's safety, Lycurgus made believe that he agreed to this plan, and asked that the child should be given to him to kill as he saw fit.

Lycurgus, having thus obtained possession of the babe, carried him to the council hall. There the child was named king; and Lycurgus promised that he would watch carefully over him, educate him well, and rule for him until he should be old and wise enough to reign alone.

While he was thus acting as ruler, Lycurgus made use of his power to bring many new customs into Sparta, and to change the laws. As he was one of the wisest men who ever lived, he knew very well that men must be good if they would be happy. He also knew that health is far better than riches; and, hoping to make the Spartans both good and healthy, he won them over little by little to obey a new set of laws, which he had made after visiting many of the neighboring countries, and learning all he could.

XXII. THE SPARTAN TRAINING.

The laws which Lycurgus drew up for the Spartans were very strict. For instance, as soon as a babe came into the world, the law ordered that the father should wrap it up in a cloak, and carry it before a council made up of some of the oldest and wisest men.

They looked at the child carefully, and if it seemed strong and healthy, and was neither crippled nor in any way deformed, they said that it might live. Then they gave it back to the father, and bade him bring up the child for the honor of his country.

If the babe was sickly or deformed, it was carried off to a mountain near by, and left alone; so that it soon died of hunger or thirst, or was eaten up by the wild beasts.

The Spartan children staid under their father's roof and in their mother's care until they were seven years old. While in the nursery, they were taught all the beautiful old Greek legends, and listened with delight to the stories of the ancient heroes, and especially to the poems of Homer telling about the war of Troy and the adventures of Ulysses.

As soon as the children had reached seven years of age, they were given over to the care of the state, and allowed to visit their parents but seldom. The boys were put in charge of chosen men, who trained them to become strong and brave; while the girls were placed under some good and wise woman, who not only taught them all they needed to know to keep house well, but also trained them to be as strong and fearless as their brothers. All Spartan boys were allowed but one rough woolen garment, which served as their sole covering by night and by day, and was of the same material in summer as in winter.

They were taught very little reading, writing, and arithmetic, but were carefully trained to recite the poems of Homer, the patriotic songs, and to accompany themselves skillfully on the lyre. They were also obliged to sing in the public chorus, and to dance gracefully at all the religious feasts.

As the Spartans were very anxious that their boys should be strong and fearless, they were taught to stand pain and fatigue without a murmur; and, to make sure that they could do so, their teachers made them go through a very severe training.

Led by one of the older boys, the little lads were often sent out for long tramps over rough and stony roads, under the hot sun; and the best boy was the one who kept up longest, in spite of bleeding feet, burning thirst, and great fatigue.

Spartan boys were allowed no beds to sleep in, lest they should become lazy and hard to please. Their only couch was a heap of rushes, which they picked on the banks of the Eu-ro´tas, a river near Sparta; and in winter they were allowed to cover these with a layer of cat-tail down to make them softer and warmer.

XXIII. THE BRAVE SPARTAN BOY.

As greedy and disobedient children were viewed at Sparta with the contempt they deserved, all the boys were trained to obey at a word, whatever the order given, and were allowed only the plainest and scantiest food.

Strange to relate, the Spartans also trained their boys to steal. They praised them when they succeeded indoing so without being found out, and punished them only when caught in the act. The reason for this queer custom was this: the people were often engaged in war, and as they had no baggage wagons following their army, and no special officer to furnish food, they had to depend entirely upon the provisions they could get on their way.

Whenever an army came in sight, the people hid not only their wealth, but also their food; and, had not the Spartan soldiers been trained to steal, they would often have suffered much from hunger when they were at war.

To test the courage of the Spartan boys, their teachers never allowed them to have a light, and often sent them out alone in the middle of the night, on errands which they had to do as best they could.

Then, too, once a year all the boys were brought to the Temple of Diana, where their courage was further tried by a severe flogging; and those who stood this whipping without a tear or moan were duly praised. The little Spartan boys were so eager to be thought brave, that it is said that some let themselves be flogged to death rather than complain.

The bravery of one of these boys was so wonderful that you will find it mentioned in nearly every Greek history you read. This little fellow had stolen a live fox, and hidden it in the bosom of his dress, on his way to school.

The imprisoned fox, hoping to escape, began to gnaw a hole in the boy's chest, and to tear his flesh with his sharp claws; but, in spite of the pain, the lad sat still, and let the fox bite him to death.

It was only when he fell lifeless to the floor that the teachers found the fox, and saw how cruelly he had torn the brave little boy to pieces. Ever since then, when boys stand pain bravely and without wincing, they have been called little Spartans, in memory of this lad.

In order that the boys should be taught to behave well under all circumstances, they were never allowed to speak except when spoken to, and then their answers were expected to be as short and exact as possible.

This style of speaking, where much was said in few words, was so usual in the whole country of Laconia, that it is still known as the laconic style.

To train them in this mode of speech, the elders daily made the boys pass an oral examination, asking them any questions they could think of. The boys had to answer promptly, briefly, and carefully; and if they failed to do so, it was considered a great disgrace.

These daily questionings were meant to sharpen their wits, strengthen their memories, and teach them how to think and decide quickly and correctly.

The Spartan youths were further taught to treat all their elders with the greatest respect; and it must have been a pretty sight to see all these manly fellows respectfully saluting all the old people they met, and even stopping their play to make way for them when they came on the street.

To strengthen their muscles, the boys were also carefully trained in gymnastics. They could handle weapons, throw heavy weights, wrestle, run with great speed, swim, jump, and ride, and were experts in all exercises which tended to make them strong, active, and well.

XXIV. PUBLIC TABLES IN SPARTA.

The Spartan men prided themselves upon living almost as plainly as the boys, and, instead of eating their meals at home with the women and children, they had a common table. Each man gave a certain amount of flour, oil, wine, vegetables, and money, just enough to provide for his share of food.

Instead of having varied and delicate dishes, they always ate about the same things; and their favorite food was a thick dark stew or soup, which they called black broth. Rich and poor were treated alike, sat side by side, and ate the same food, which was intended to make them equally strong and able to serve their country.

The girls and women never came to these public tables; but the boys were given a seat there as soon as they had learned their first and most important lesson, obedience.

When the boys came into the public dining hall for the first time, the oldest man present called them to him, and, pointing to the door, solemnly warned them that nothing said inside the walls was ever to be repeated without.

Then, while the boys took their places and ate without speaking a word, the old men talked freely of all they pleased, sure that Spartan lads would never be mean enough to repeat anything they said, and trusting to their honor.

Although the Spartans had wine upon their table, they were a very temperate people, and drank only a very little with each meal. To show the boys what a horrible thing drunkenness is, and the sure result of too much drinking, the old men sometimes gave them an object lesson.

They sent for one of the meanest Helots or slaves, and purposely gave him plenty of wine. He was encouraged to go on drinking until he sank on the floor in a drunken sleep. Then the old men would point him out to the boys, and explain to them that a man who has drunk too much is unworthy of the love or esteem of his fellow-creatures, and is in many ways worse than a beast.

The Spartan boys, thus early warned of the evils of drinking, were careful to take but very little wine, and to keep their heads quite clear, so that they might always be considered men, and might never disgrace themselves as they had seen the Helots do.

When the boys had passed through the first course of training, they in turn became the teachers and leaders of the smaller lads, and thus served their country until they were old enough to go to war. When they left for their first campaign, all the people came out to see them off, and each mother gave her son his shield, saying,—

"Come back with it or on it."

By this she meant "Come home honorably, bearing your shield, thus showing that you have never thrown it away to save yourself by flight; or die so bravely that your companions will bring back your body resting on your shield, to give you a glorious burial."

XXV. LAWS OF LYCURGUS.

The Spartan girls, who were brought up by the women, were, like the boys, taught to wrestle, run, and swim, and to take part in gymnastics of all kinds, until they too became very strong and supple, and could stand almost any fatigue.

They were also taught to read, write, count, sing, play, and dance; to spin, weave, and dye; and to do all kinds of woman's work. In short, they were expected to be strong, intelligent, and capable, so that when they married they might help their husbands, and bring up their children sensibly. At some public festivals the girls strove with one another in various games, which were witnessed only by their fathers and mothers and the other married people of the city. The winners in these contests were given beautiful prizes, which were much coveted.

Lycurgus hoped to make the Spartans a strong and good people. To hinder the kings from doing anything wrong, he had the people choose five men, called ephors, to watch over and to advise them.

Then, knowing that great wealth is not desirable, Lycurgus said that the Spartans should use only iron money. All the Spartan coins were therefore bars of iron, so heavy that a yoke of oxen and a strong cart were needed to carry a sum equal to one hundred dollars from one spot to another. Money was so bulky that it could neither be hidden nor stolen; and no one cared to make a fortune, since it required a large space to stow away even a small sum.

When Charilaus, the infant king, had grown up, Lycurgus prepared to go away. Before he left the town, he called all the citizens together, reminded them of all he had done to

A Dancing Girl.

make them a great people, and ended by asking every man present to swear to obey the laws until he came back.

The Spartans were very grateful for all he had done for them, so they gladly took this oath, and Lycurgus left the place. Some time after, he came back to Greece; but, hearing that the Spartans were thriving under the rules he had laid down, he made up his mind never to visit Sparta again.

It was thus that the Spartans found themselves bound by solemn oath to obey Lycurgus' laws forever; and as long as they remembered this promise, they were a thriving and happy people.

XXVI. THE MESSENIAN WAR.

Not very far from Sparta, and next to Laconia, was a country called Mes-se´ni-a, which was much more fertile, and had long been occupied by a kindred race descended from Le´lex, brother of Lacedæmon.

When the Spartans found out that the Mes-se´ni-an fields were more fruitful than their own, they longed to have them, and anxiously watched for some excuse to make war against the Messenians and win their land. It was not long before they found one.

There was a temple on the boundary of Messenia and Laconia, where the people of both countries used to assemble on certain days to offer up sacrifices to the gods. The Messenian lads, seeing the beauty of the Spartan girls, and longing to have such strong, handsome, and intelligent wives, once carried off a few of them into their own country, and refused to give them up again. The Spartans, indignant at this conduct, flew to arms, and one night, led by their king, attacked the Messenian town of Am-phe´a.

As no one expected them, they soon became masters of the place, and in their anger killed all the inhabitants. The other Messenians, hearing of this cruel deed, quickly made ready to fight, and bravely began the struggle which is known as the First Messenian War.

Although very brave, the Messenians had not been as well trained as the Spartans, and could not drive them back. On the contrary, they were themselves driven from place to place, until they were forced to take refuge in the fortified city of I-tho´me. Here they were shut in with their king, Aristodemus, who was a proud and brave man.

Ithome was built high up on a rock, so steep that the Spartan soldiers could not climb it, and so high that they could not even shoot their arrows into the town.

The Messenians, hoping to keep this place of refuge, kept a sharp lookout, and, whenever the Spartans made any attempt to climb the rocks, they rolled great blocks of stone down upon them.

All went well as long as the food lasted, but the time came when the Messenians in Ithome had nothing to eat. Some of their bravest men tried to go down into the valley in search of provisions; but, as they were attacked by the Spartans, they could not bring the hungry people much to eat.

When Aristodemus saw that the people would all die of hunger unless some way were found to get food, he consulted an oracle, in order to find out what it was best for him to do. The oracle answered that a battle should be fought, and promised the victory to the king who offered his daughter in sacrifice to the gods.

When Aristodemus heard this answer, he shuddered with fear; for, although he knew that his ancestors had offered up human victims on their altars, he loved his only daughter too well to give her up.

For some time longer, therefore, he resisted every attack, and tried to think of some other way to save his people. At last, however, seeing that they would all die unless something were done, he sacrificed the child he loved so well.

The Messenians were touched by his generosity, and by his readiness to do all in his power to save them. They felt sure that the gods would now give them the victory, and rushed out of the town and into the Spartan camp. Their attack was so sudden, and they fought with such fury, that they soon killed three hundred Spartans and one of their kings.

This battle did not, as they had hoped, end the war, which went on for several years. At last Aristodemus, despairing of victory, went to his beloved daughter's tomb, and there killed himself.

When he was dead, the city of Ithome fell into the hands of the Spartans. They treated the conquered Messenians with great cruelty, made them all slaves, and were as unkind to them as they had been to the Helots.

XXVII. THE MUSIC OF TYRTÆUS.

After suffering great tortures under the Spartan yoke for forty long years, the Messenians began to plan a revolt.

One of their princes, Ar-is-tom´e-nes, a man of unusual bravery, made up his mind to free the unhappy people, and to ruin the proud city of Sparta, which had caused them so much suffering.

He therefore secretly assembled all the Messenians, and, when his plans were ready, began to war openly against the Spartans, whom he defeated in several battles.

With his small army, he even pressed forward toward the city of Sparta, and camped within sight of its dwellings. The Spartan women could thus see a very unusual sight,—the light of the enemies' fires.

To frighten the Spartans still more, Aristomenes went secretly into the city one dark night, stole into the principal temple, and there hung up the arms he had taken during the war.

These weapons were arranged so as to form what the Greeks called a trophy, and right under them Aristomenes boldly wrote his name in letters so large that all could see it.

When morning dawned, and the Spartans came as usual into the temple to offer up their morning prayer and sacrifice, they were astonished and dismayed at the sight of this trophy. Aristomenes' bravery was so great that they despaired of conquering him without divine aid, and so they sent to ask an oracle what they should do.

The oracle answered that the Spartans would be victorious if they marched to war under the command of an Athenian general. Now, the Spartans were a proud people, and did not like to ask aid of any one; but they made up their minds to obey this command, and so sent a messenger to Athens to ask for a good leader.

Whether the Athenians, who were well known for their love of joking, wished to make fun of the Spartans, or whether they wanted to show them that the bodily beauty and strength which the Spartans prized so highly was not everything, no one now knows. The fact is, however, that the Athenians sent the Spartans a poor, lame schoolmaster, called Tyr-tæ´us, to lead them in battle. This man had never handled a weapon in his life, and the Spartans were very angry when he placed himself at their head with a lyre instead of a sword; but when he suddenly began to sing one of those war songs which make one's blood tingle, it roused their patriotism to such a point that all were ready to conquer or die, and their scorn was soon changed to deep admiration.

Fired by these patriotic songs, and by the stirring music the lame schoolmaster played, the Spartans fought better than ever before, overcame the Messenians, and came home in triumph with their prisoners, among whom was the brave Aristomenes.

As it was then usual to put all prisoners of war to death, the Spartans threw all the Messenians down into a horrible pit called the Ce´a-das. This was a dark hole of great depth, and its sides were all covered with jagged rocks, against which the prisoners were dashed to pieces long before they reached the bottom.

The Messenians were cast into this place one after another, Aristomenes being thrown in last of all, so that he might have the sorrow of seeing his companions die. Of course, this was very cruel, but the Spartans had been brought up to think this mode of getting rid of their enemies quite right; and when they had thus killed them, they cheerfully went back to the city and celebrated their victory.

XXVIII. ARISTOMENES' ESCAPE.

Although the Spartans thought that Aristomenes was dead, they were greatly mistaken. By some miracle he had not struck against any of the sharp, jagged rocks, but, falling upon the heap of his dead companions, had reached the bottom of the Ceadas unhurt.

There was apparently no way out of this pit except by the opening at the top, through which a bit of sky could be seen; and Aristomenes soon found that the sides were so steep that it was impossible to reach the opening. He therefore went off to one side, away from the heap of dead, and sat down on a stone in that cold, damp, and dark place. There he drew his cloak over his head to wait patiently until he should starve to death. Three days had thus been spent in this place, and his strength was already fast failing, when he suddenly felt a warm breath on his hand.

He softly drew aside his cloak, and, now that his eyes were used to the darkness, he dimly saw a fox prowling around him, and sniffing his clothes suspiciously.

Gently wrapping his cloak around his hand to protect it from the fox's sharp teeth, Aristomenes caught the animal firmly by the tail. Then, in spite of all its efforts to get away, he held it tight; and when it started off, he followed its lead.

As he had shrewdly suspected, the fox knew a way out of the horrible place. All at once it slipped into a hole; and Aristomenes, seeing a little light at the end of this, let the fox go. With the help of a sharp stone, he soon made the fox's hole big enough to crawl through, and quickly made his way back to the Messenians.

You can imagine how happy they were to see the beloved chief whom they thought dead, and how tenderly they cared for him until he was well and strong again. They never tired of hearing the story of his fall, imprisonment, and escape; and when he proposed to lead them once more against the Spartans, they gladly promised to help him.

In spite of all Aristomenes' courage, however, Messenia finally fell into the hands of the Spartans, and the Second Messenian War came to an end. All the people who wished to escape slavery or death left their native country, and went to Italy or Sicily, where they founded Greek colonies.

The cities that they built soon became very powerful, and one of them they named Mes-si´na in honor of their native land. This city still stands, as you will see by looking at your maps; and near it is the strait of the same name, which separates Sicily from Italy.

XXIX. THE OLYMPIC GAMES.

Northwest of Sparta, in the country called E´lis and in the city of O-lym´pi-a, rose a beautiful temple for the worship of Ju´pi-ter (or Zeus), the principal god of the Greeks. This temple was said to have been built by Hercules, the great hero from whom, as you remember, all the

Heraclidæ claimed to be descended.

According to the legends, Hercules was a son of the god Jupiter, and had ordered that a great festival should be held here every four years in honor of his divine father.

The Temple at Olympia.

For the purpose of attracting all the neighboring people to the temple at Olympia, Hercules founded many athletic games, such as wrestling, stone and spear throwing, foot, horse, and chariot races, boxing, swimming, and the like.

Hercules himself was present at the first of these festivals, and acted as umpire of the games, rewarding the victors by giving them crowns of wild olive leaves. This custom had been kept up ever since, and the Greek youths considered this simple crown the finest prize which could be given.

As the Spartans were great athletes, they soon took important parts in the Olympic games, won most of the prizes, and claimed the honor of defending the temple at Olympia in all times of danger.

All the people who went to Olympia to witness the games laid some precious offering before the shrines, so that the temple came to be noted for its beauty and wealth. Painters and sculptors, too, further adorned it with samples of their skill, and it soon contained numerous gems of art.

The most precious of all was a statue representing Jupiter, which was the work of the renowned sculptor Phid'i-as. This statue was more than forty feet high; and, while the god himself was carved out of pure white ivory, his hair, beard, and garments were made of gold, and his eyes of the brightest jewels.

The temple and grove were further adorned with a great many statues representing the other gods and all the prize winners, for it was customary to place a life-sized statue of each of them in this beautiful place.

During the celebration of the Olympic games many sacrifices were offered up to the gods, and there were many religious processions in their honor. Poets and artists, as well as athletes, were in the habit of hastening thither on every occasion; for there were contests in poetry and song, and the people were anxious to hear and see all the new works.

Between the games, therefore, the poets recited their poems, the musicians sang their songs, the historians read their histories, and the story-tellers told their choicest tales, to amuse the vast crowd which had come there from all parts of Greece, and even from the shores of Italy and Asia Minor.

As the games were held every four years, the people eagerly looked forward to their coming, and soon began to reckon time by them. It was therefore usual to say that such and such a thing happened in the first, second, or third year of the fifth, tenth, or seventieth O-lym'pi-ad, as the case might be.

Soon even the historians began to use this way of dating important events; and by counting four years for each Olympiad, as the time between the games was called, we can find out exactly when the chief events in Greek history took place.

Although the Olympic games were probably held many times before this system of counting was begun, and before any good record was kept, we can trace them back to 774 B.C.

For one thousand years after that, the name of each victor was carefully written down; and it was only about three centuries after Christ that the Olympic records ceased. Then the games came to an end, to the sorrow of all the Greeks.

Several attempts have since been made to revive these games; but all proved fruitless until the Greek king arranged to renew them in 1896. In that year a great festival was held, not at Olympia, but in the city of Athens.

Besides some of the old-fashioned Greek games, there were bicycle and hurdle races, shooting matches, and contests in jumping. People from all parts of the world went to see them in as large numbers as they went to Olympia in the olden times.

The victors in the games, who belonged to many different nations, received medals, and wreaths of wild olive and laurel leaves; but the people did not wear crowns of flowers as formerly, nor offer sacrifices to the old gods, for Greece is now a Christian country.

XXX. MILO OF CROTON.

Among the athletes whose statues were to be seen at Olympia was Mi'lo, a man of Cro'ton, one of the Greek colonies in Italy. This man was remarkable for his great strength, and could carry very heavy weights. In order to develop his muscle and become strong, he had trained himself from a boy, and had practiced carrying burdens until he could lift more than any other man of his time.

We are told that he was so earnest in his efforts to become strong, that he daily carried a pet calf, gradually increasing the distance. As the calf grew larger, Milo became stronger, and his muscles became so powerful that he could carry the animal with ease when it became a full-sized ox.

To please his companions and show them what he could do, Milo once carried an ox for several miles, andthen, feeling hungry, killed it with one blow of his fist, cooked it, and ate it all at a single meal. On another occasion, Milo was sitting with several companions in a rather tumble-down house. All at once he noticed that the roof was falling in. He stretched up his great arms, spread out his hands, and held the roof up until all his companions had run out of the house.

Milo's hands were so strong that when he seized a chariot, even with one hand only, four horses could not make it stir until he let it go. Of course, Milo was very proud of his great strength, which, however, proved unlucky for him, and caused his death.

One day when he was very old, Milo wandered out alone into a forest where some woodcutters had been at work. The men had gone away, leaving their wedges in an unusually large tree trunk.

Milo, remembering his former strength, gazed for a moment at the tree, and then, feeling sure that he could easily pull it apart, he slipped his fingers into the crack. At his first effort the tree parted a little, and the wedges fell out; but the two halves, instead of splitting apart, suddenly came together again, and Milo found his hands held fast.

In vain he struggled, in vain he called. He could neither wrench himself free nor attract any one's attention. Night came on, and soon the wild beasts of the forest began to creep out of their dens.

They found the captive athlete, and, springing upon him, tore him to pieces, for he could not defend himself, in spite of all his boasted strength.

XXXI. THE JEALOUS ATHLETE.

Near the statue of Milo of Croton stood that of The-ag´e-nes, another noted athlete, who lived many years after Milo. He too had defeated every rival. He was the winner of many prizes, and all envied him his strength and renown.

One of the men in particular, whom he had defeated in the games, was jealous of him, and of the honors which he had won. This man, instead of trying to overcome these wicked feelings, used to steal daily into the temple to view his rival's statue, and mutter threats and curses against it.

In his anger, he also gave the pedestal an angry shake every night, hoping that some harm would befall the statue. One evening, when this jealous man had jostled the image of Theagenes a little more roughly than usual, the heavy marble toppled and fell, crushing him to death beneath its weight.

When the priests came into the temple the next day, and found the man's dead body under the great statue, they were very much surprised. The judges assembled, as was the custom when a crime of any kind had been committed, to decide what had caused his death.

As it was usual in Greece to hold judgment over lifeless as well as over living things, the statue of Theagenes was brought into court, and accused and found guilty of murder.

The judges then said, that, as the statue had committed a crime, it deserved to be punished, and so theycondemned it to be cast into the sea and drowned. This sentence had scarcely been executed, when a plague broke out in Greece; and when the frightened people consulted an oracle to find out how it could be checked, they learned that it would not cease until the statue of Theagenes had been set up on its pedestal again. The superstitious Greeks believed these words, fished the statue up out of the sea, and placed it again in Olympia. As the plague stopped shortly after this, they all felt sure that it was because they had obeyed the oracle, and they ever after looked upon the statue with great awe.

XXXII. THE GIRLS' GAMES.

Although the women and girls were not often allowed to appear in public, or to witness certain of the Olympic games, there were special days held sacred to them, when the girls also strove for prizes.

They too ran races; and it must have been a pretty sight to see all those healthy, happy girls running around the stadium, as the foot-race course was called.

One of these races was called the torch race, for each runner carried a lighted torch in her hand. All were allowed to try to put out each other's light; and the prize was given to the maiden who first reached the goal with her torch aflame, or to the one who kept hers burning longest.

The prize for the girls was the same as that given to the boys; but the boys took part in more games, and were present in greater numbers, than the girls, and their victories were praised much more than those of their sisters.

A Torch Race.

The crowd of people watching the games often grew so excited that they carried the victor all around the grounds on their shoulders, while Olympia fairly re-echoed with their cries of joy.

We are also told that one old man called Chi′lo was so happy when his son laid at his feet the crowns he had just won, that he actually died of joy, thus turning his son's happiness into bitter grief.

While all the foot races took place in the stadium, the horse and chariot races were held in the hippodrome, and excited the greatest interest. There were two-, four-, and eight-horse races; and, as the horses were sometimes unruly, the chariots were liable to be overturned. Thus at times a number of horses would fall in a heap, and lie struggling and kicking in the dust, which added to the general excitement.

XXXIII. THE BLOODY LAWS OF DRACO.

You have already learned that Athens was one of the greatest cities of ancient Greece, and that after the heroic self-sacrifice of Codrus the inhabitants would not allow any one to bear the name of king.

The sons of Codrus were named archons, or rulers for life,—an office which was at first handed down from father to son, but which soon became elective; that is to say, all the people voted for and elected their own rulers. Then nine archons were chosen at once, but they kept their office for only one year.

As these men received no pay for serving the state, only the richest citizens could accept the office; and thus Athens, from a monarchy, or country ruled by a king, became an oligarchy, or state ruled by the rich and noble citizens.

As the rich thus held the reins of the government, they often used their power to oppress the poor, and this gave rise to many quarrels. Little by little the two parties, the rich and the poor, grew to hate each other so much that it was decided that a new code or set of laws should be made, and that they should be obeyed by all alike.

A severe archon called Dra´co was chosen to draw up these new laws (602 B.C.); and he made them so strict and cruel that the least sin was punished as if it had been a crime, and a man was sentenced to be hanged for stealing even a cabbage.

When the Athenians heard these new laws, they were frightened. Such severity had never been known before; and one and all said that the laws had been written in blood instead of ink. Some of the citizens, hoping to make Draco change them, asked why he had named such a terrible punishment for so small a crime as the theft of a cabbage. Draco sternly replied that a person who stole even the smallest thing was dishonest, and deserved death; and that, as he knew of no severer punishment, he could not inflict one for the greater crimes.

The Athenians had all promised to obey Draco's laws, so they were obliged to submit for a short time. Then, driven wild by their strictness, rich and poor rose up, drove the unhappy lawmaker out of the city, and forced him to go to the neighboring Island of Æ-gi´na. Here Draco spent all the rest of his life.

The people were now in a state of great uncertainty. The laws of Draco were too severe, but they had no others to govern the city. While they were hesitating, not knowing what to do, Cy´lon, an Athenian citizen, tried to make himself king.

His first move was to gather together a few of his friends, and go secretly to the Acropolis, or fortress of Athens, which he took by surprise. Now that he was master of the fortress, he tried to force the Athenians to recognize him as their king, but this they stoutly refused to do.

Instead of yielding, the Athenians armed themselves, met the rebels in a bloody battle, and killed Cylon himself in the midst of the fight.

As their leader was now dead, and they feared the anger of their fellow-citizens, Cylon's friends fled in haste to the temple of the goddess Athene. Once inside the sacred building, they felt quite safe; for no person could be killed in a temple, or be taken out of it by force.

Although they had neither food nor drink, the rebels refused to leave the temple, until the archon Meg´a-cles, fearing that they would die there, and thus defile the temple, promised to do them no harm if they would only come out.

The rebels did not quite trust to this promise, so they came out of the temple holding a small cord, one end of which was fastened to the statue of the goddess. They were thus still under her protection, and any one touching them would be guilty of a great crime.

When the men reached the street at the bottom of the hill where the temple stood, the cord to which they were all clinging suddenly broke. Megacles, the first to notice this, said that the goddess refused to protect the rebels any longer, and gave orders to kill the unhappy men.

XXXIV. THE LAWS OF SOLON.

Shortly after the death of Cylon and the murder of his followers, a great many troubles came upon the city of Athens. The people were frightened, and soon the friends of Cylon began to whisper that the gods were surely punishing the Athenians, and especially Megacles, for breaking his promise.

This report spread throughout the city. The terrified people assembled, and voted to exile Megacles and all his family, the Alc-mæ-on´i-dæ. Such was the fury of the Athenians against the archon whose crime had brought misfortunes upon them, that they even dug up the bones of his ancestors, and had them carried beyond the boundary of Attica.

The city had been defiled by the crime which Megacles had committed, and the people felt that they would never be prosperous again until Athens had been purified; but the great question was to find a man holy enough to perform the ceremony.

After much talking, they decided to send for Ep-i-men´i-des, and to ask him to purify the city. This man, when a mere lad, once went into a cave near his native town, and there laid himself down to sleep. Instead of taking an ordinary nap, however, he slept fifty-eight years, without awakening or undergoing any change. When he came out of the cave, where he fancied he had spent only a few hours, he was surprised to find everything new and strange to him.

His relatives had all died, no one knew him, and it was only after some time had passed that he found out that he had slept fifty-eight years at a stretch. This man was a poet of note, and, as he had enjoyed so long a sleep, the people thought that he was a favorite of the gods.

When the Athenians asked him to purify the town, he came to do so; but when the ceremonies were ended, he refused to accept any of the rich gifts which the people offered him as reward. Instead, he humbly begged them to give him a twig of the sacred olive tree which they said Athene herself had planted on the Acropolis.

Their troubles having now ceased, the Athenians began to think of making another and less severe code of laws. This time they chose as lawmaker a wise man called So´lon, a descendant of the noble Codrus; and he soon consented to tell them what to do.

Solon was a studious and thoughtful man, and had acquired much of his wisdom by traveling, and by learning all he could from the people he visited. He knew so much that he was called a sage, and he loved to meet and talk with wise people.

Solon changed many of Draco's severe laws, arranged that the farmers and poor people should no longer be treated badly by the rich, and even took care of the slaves. He also gave the Athenians a court of law called A-re-op´a-gus. Here there were jurymen to judge all criminals; and here, for the first time, an accused person was allowed to speak in his own defense.

When a man was accused of any wrongdoing, he was brought before this jury, who sat under the open sky at night. No light was provided, and the whole trial was carried on in the dark, so that the jury should not be influenced by the good or bad looks of the prisoner, but should judge merely from what was proved about him.

If the accused person was found guilty, he was also sentenced and executed in the dark, so that the bright sun god, riding across the sky in his golden chariot, should not be offended by the sad sight of a man dying for his misdeeds.

Every citizen of Athens, whether rich or poor, was allowed to vote; and as a salary was now paid to the men who helped govern the city, even a man of small means, if elected to the Tribunal, could afford to give his time to public duties.

By Solon's order the people were encouraged to talk matters over in public in the market place; and, as the Athenians were fond of making speeches, many of them became very eloquent.

Solon saw that his reforms were likely to work all the better if they were fairly tried, and if he were not there to see how the people did. He therefore made the Athenians promise to obey his laws for ten years, and again set out on his travels.

XXXV. THE FIRST PLAYS.

In the days of Solon, men were often to be seen wandering around the streets during the festival of Di-o-ny´sus, god of wine. They were clad in goatskins, were smeared with the dregs of wine, and danced and sang rude songs in honor of their god.

Theater of Dionysus.

These songs were called tragedies, which in Greek means "goat songs," because the goat was sacred to the god whom they thus worshiped. The people were greatly amused by the rude songs and dances of these worshipers of Dionysus, and crowds gathered about them to listen to their singing and to watch their antics.

Thes'pis, a Greek of great intelligence, noticed how popular these amusements were, and to please the public taste he set up the first rude theater. In the beginning it was only a few boards raised on trestles to form a sort of stage in the open air; but Thespis soon built a booth, so that the actors, when not on the stage, could be hidden from public view.

The first plays, as already stated, were very simple, and consisted of popular songs rudely acted. Little by little, however, the plays became more and more elaborate, and the actors tried to represent some of the tales which the story-tellers had told.

Some people did not approve of this kind of amusement; and among them was Solon, who said that Thespis was teaching the Athenians to love a lie, because they liked the plays, which, of course, were not true.

In spite of Solon's displeasure, the actors went on playing, and soon the best poets began to write works for the stage. The actors became more and more skillful, and had many spectators, although no women were allowed on the stage, their parts being taken by men.

Finally, to make room for the ever-increasing number of theater goers, a huge amphitheater was built. It was so large, we are told, that there were seats for thirty thousand spectators. These seats were in semicircular rows or tiers, of which there were one hundred, rising one above another. The lowest row of all, near the orchestra, was composed of sixty huge marble chairs. The amphitheater was open to the sky, the stage alone being covered with a roof; and all the plays were given by daylight. The ruins of this building, which is known as the Theater of Dionysus, were dug out in 1862, and are now often visited by people who go to Athens.

Sophocles.

The Greek actors soon dressed in costume, and all wore masks expressing the various emotions they wished to represent. The principal parts of the play were recited; but from time to time singers came on the stage, and chanted parts of the play in chorus.

Some of these plays were so sad that the whole audience was melted to tears; others were so funny that the people shouted with laughter. When you learn Greek, you will be able to read the grand tragedies which were written by Æs'chy-lus, Soph'o-cles, and Eu-rip'i-des, and the comedies or funny plays of Ar-is-toph'a-nes.

XXXVI. THE TYRANT PISISTRATUS.

Not very long after Solon had given the new laws to the Athenians, the two political parties of the city again began to quarrel. One of these parties was composed wholly of rich men and nobles, or *aristoi*, from which Greek word is formed our English word "aristocrat;" the other party included the farmers and poor people, or *demos*, the Greek term which has given rise to the word "democrat."

Among the aristocrats, or nobles, there was a nephew of Solon called Pi-sis´tra-tus. He was very rich; but, instead of upholding his own party, he seemed to scorn the rich, and always sided with the poor. To make friends with the democrats, he pretended to obey the laws with the greatest care, and addressed every man with the utmost politeness.

Once, having killed a man by accident, Pisistratus came of his own free will before the judges of the Areopagus, confessed his crime, and was so humble that he quite disarmed the anger of the people.

As soon as he felt quite sure that he had won many friends among the poor, Pisistratus appeared one day in the market place, covered with blood, which flowed from slight wounds which he had made upon his own body.

His polite manners and kindly words had been only a pretense, however; and he was not only a hypocrite, but also a liar. So he now said that the aristocrats had tried to kill him because he was the friend of the people.

In proof of these words, he pointed to his wounds. The poorer Athenians, who believed him, were very indignant, and began to talk angrily about the wicked nobles, who had hurt Pisistratus only because he was ready to help them.

When Pisistratus cried out that his life was no longer safe, all the democrats exclaimed that they would protect him; and, as they had the right of voting, they then and there said that he should have a bodyguard of fifty armed men to protect him.

Pisistratus pretended to be very grateful for this favor, and, under pretext of choosing his bodyguard, engaged a great number of soldiers. When his plans were all ready, he took possession of the Acropolis by force.

The people now found out, but too late, that Pisistratus had deceived them only to get more power; and that, thanks to the guard they had voted him, he had become master of the town, and held the reins of the government.

The Athenians did not long remain angry with their former favorite, however; for he did all he could to make them happy, and ruled them very wisely. He improved the city by building magnificent temples and other public buildings, and made a great aqueduct, so that the people could have plenty of pure water to drink.

Pisistratus also laid out a public park, the Ly-ce´um, just outside the city walls, so that the Athenians could go there, and enjoy the cool shade of the groves he had planted.

Then he began to collect all the poems of Homer, had them carefully written down, and placed them in apublic library, so that the Greeks could read them whenever they pleased. Until then these poems had only been recited, and no written copy existed. Pisistratus, therefore, did a very good work in thus keeping for our enjoyment the greatest epic poems ever composed.

As Pisistratus ruled just as he pleased, without consulting the Tribunal or people, he has been called a tyrant. This word in those days meant "supreme ruler;" but as many of those who followed him made a bad use of their power, and were cruel and grasping, its meaning soon changed, and the word now means "a selfish and unkind ruler."

XXXVII. THE TYRANT'S INSULT.

While Pisistratus was thus governing Athens to suit himself, Solon was traveling in Asia, where he met several interesting persons of whom you will hear in ancient history.

Solon had gone away for ten years, hoping that the Athenians would strictly obey his laws. During that time he had no news of his native land; for there were no post offices or newspapers in those days, and people neither wrote nor received letters except when something very important happened.

On coming back to Athens, Solon was very sorry to learn that it was Pisistratus, his own kinsman, who had taken the power of the archons; but when he saw how wisely Pisistratus governed the people, and how careful he was to make them happy and improve them, he freely forgave him, and remained on good terms with him until he died.

Pisistratus went on ruling the Athenians for thirty-three years, and when he died they mourned him greatly. In their grief for their loss, they allowed his sons, Hip'-pi-as and Hip-par'chus, to succeed him, without raising any objections.

These young men were very careful at first to follow their father's good example; but they soon began to neglect business for pleasure, and, instead of thinking of the people's good, they spent much of their time in feasting and drinking.

In those days there dwelt at Athens two young men named Har-mo'di-us and A-ris-to-gi'ton. They were intimate friends, and were loved by all on account of their good qualities, and more especially because they were so anxious to increase the glory and prosperity of their native city.

Harmodius had a sister who was as good as she was beautiful: so the people, hoping to please him, chose her to carry a basket of flowers in the great religious procession which took place in Athens every year.

One of the tyrants, Hipparchus, was very jealous of Harmodius, because the people loved him so much. He therefore tried to annoy the young man in every way; and when he heard that his sister had been chosen to bear the flowers, he rudely forbade her presence at the feast.

This was a great insult, for none but wicked women were forbidden to appear; and, as Hipparchus had thus publicly disgraced the girl, her brother was very angry.

His friend, Aristogiton, was as angry as he; and the two young men, consulting together, decided that as long as these men ruled, the Athenians would be treated badly, and that it would be well to get rid of them soon.

XXXVIII. DEATH OF THE CONSPIRATORS.

Harmodius and Aristogiton, having decided to get rid of the tyrants, told their plans to a few of their friends. Secret meetings were held at the house of a brave lady called Le-æ'na ("the lioness"), who was the only woman in the plot.

As the Athenians were in the habit of attending the feast in armor, the young men waited until then to carry out their plans. They mingled with the crowd, found a good place near the tyrants, and all at once drew their swords from their scabbards and attacked their enemies.

Harmodius was so quick that he managed to kill Hipparchus; but, before his companions could join and protect him, he was cut down by the tyrants' guards.

Aristogiton, his friend, rushed forward to save him, but was made prisoner, and dragged before Hippias, who bade him tell the names of his companions. The young man at first refused to speak; but after a while, pretending to yield, he named some of the tyrants' friends who were helping him oppress the Athenians.

The tyrant, in dismay, sent for the accused, and had them and Aristogiton killed without trial. When he found out his mistake, he again tried to learn the names of the real conspirators. He knew that Harmodius and Aristogiton had often visited Leæna: so he had her imprisoned and tortured, to make her tell the names of the conspirators, because he wanted to kill them all as he had killed

Aristogiton.

The brave woman, knowing that the lives of several young men depended upon her, and that a single word might cause their death, resolved not to utter a sound. In spite of the most awful tortures, she therefore kept her mouth tightly closed; and when she was finally set free, they found that she had bitten off her tongue for fear of betraying her friends.

Poor Leæna did not live long after this; and when she died, she was buried in a beautiful tomb, over which her friends put the image of a lioness without a tongue, to remind the people of her courage.

The Athenians were very sorry for her death, and mourned the brave youths Harmodius and Aristogiton for a long time; but the tyranny of the son of Pisistratus daily grew more cruel and disagreeable.

XXXIX. HIPPIAS DRIVEN OUT OF ATHENS.

Four years passed thus, and the Athenians were hoping that the time would soon come when they could get rid of Hippias. They were only too glad, therefore, when they at last found a way to drive him out of the town.

Delphi.

You must remember how Megacles had killed the men who came out of Athene's temple clinging to the cord they had fastened to her statue. Megacles, as you know, had been banished from Athens with all his family (the Alcmæonidæ) on account of this crime, but he had always hoped to be allowed to return.

Meanwhile the beautiful temple at Delphi had been burned to the ground, and the people were very anxious to rebuild it. They therefore voted a certain sum of money for this purpose; and, as the Alcmæonidæ offered to do the work for the least pay, the contract was given to them.

The Alcmæonidæ faithfully carried out the plans, and used the money; but, instead of building the temple of brick, they made it of pure white marble, paying for the more costly material themselves.

The priests of Delphi were so pleased with the handsome new building, and with the generosity of the builders, that they were eager to do them a good turn. So, knowing that the Alcmæonidæ wanted to get back to Athens, they told the Spartans who came to consult the oracle, that Hippias should be driven away, and the Alcmæonidæ allowed to return to their native city.

As the people believed all the oracle said, the Spartans armed at once, and, helped by the Alcmæonidæ, began to make war against the Athenians. By a clever trick, they soon managed to capture the family of Hippias, and they refused to set them free unless the tyrant left Athens forever.

Thus forced to give in, Hippias left Athens, and withdrew with his family to Asia Minor. Here he spent all his time in trying to persuade the different cities to make war against Athens, offering to lead their armies, for he still hoped to regain his lost power.

The Athenians, delighted at the expulsion of the Pis-is-trat'i-dæ, as the driving-away of Hippias and his family is called in history, now dared to make statues in honor of their favorites Harmodius and Aristogiton, and openly expressed their regret that these brave young men had not lived to see their native city free.

Many songs were composed to celebrate the patriotism of the two friends; and these were sung on all public occasions, to encourage other youths to follow their example, lead good and virtuous lives, and be ready at any time to die, if need be, for the sake of their native land.

Leæna, too, received much praise, for the Athenian women never forgot how bravely she had endured torture rather than betray the men who had trusted her.

The Alcmæonidæ, having thus found their way back into the city, now began to play an important part in the government; and Clis'the-nes, their leader, urged the Athenians to obey again the laws which had been made by Solon.

These were slightly changed, however, so as to give more power to the people; and the government thus became more democratic than ever. Then, too, Clisthenes said that there should always be ten Athenian generals who should hold supreme command each for a day in turn.

He also made a law, to the effect that no man should be driven out of the city unless there were six thousand votes in favor of his exile. These votes were given in a strange way.

When a man was so generally disliked that his departure seemed best, all the Athenians assembled in the market place. Then each voter received a shell (Greek, *ostrakon*), and dropped it into a place made for that purpose. All in favor of banishment wrote upon their shells the name of the man they wished to exile. The others left theirs blank.

When all the votes had thus been cast, the shells were carefully counted, and, if six thousand bore the name of the same man, he was driven out of the city, or ostracized, as it was called from the name of the shell, for ten years.

XL. THE GREAT KING.

Hippias, the exiled tyrant of Athens, as we have already seen, had taken up his abode in Asia Minor, where he made several unsuccessful attempts to regain his power.

The Greek cities were not ready to help him, however, so he tried to get another ally. Now, the greatest ruler in Asia Minor was Da-ri'us, the king who won his throne by the aid of his horse and groom, as you will see in ancient history.

He was a powerful monarch,—so powerful that the Greeks, who had built cities all along the coast of Asia Minor, in the country called Ionia, never spoke of him except as "The Great King."

Darius' kingdom was so large that it was quite impossible for one person to govern it without help. He therefore divided it into satrapies, or provinces, each of which was under the care of a satrap, or governor. These men received their orders from the king, saw that they were obeyed in all the territory under their care, and kept Darius informed of all that was going on.

The Great King generally dwelt at Ec-bat'a-na, a city surrounded by seven walls, each painted in a different but very bright color. Inside the seventh and last wall stood the palace and treasure house, which was fairly overflowing with gold and precious stones.

As there were armed soldiers at every gate in the seven walls, only the people to whom the king was willing to grant an audience could enter.

Now, although so secluded, Darius knew perfectly well all that was happening in every part of his kingdom, and even in the neighboring states; for his satraps sent him messengers daily to report all the news, and he had many paid spies, whose duty it was to tell him all they knew.

He was therefore one of the first Eastern rulers who heard of the revolt of the Athenians; and soon after this he learned that Hippias had come to Asia, and was trying to induce the Greek cities to make war against the Athenians.

When Hippias arrived at Ecbatana in search of aid, he could not immediately see the king, but was obliged to send in a message written on a waxen tablet. This passed from hand to hand, and finally reached Darius, who, recognizing the name at the bottom of the request, graciously said that he would receive the exiled tyrant of Athens.

XLI. HIPPIAS VISITS DARIUS.

Hippias was led by one of the officers of the king's household past all the guards, who respectfully made way for him, and was brought into the most magnificent dwelling he had ever seen. All the walls were covered with silken hangings of the richest dyes, and the furniture sparkled with gold and precious stones.

After passing through many rooms, where he saw richly dressed courtiers, and guards with jeweled weapons, Hippias was finally brought into a great audience chamber, at one end of which hung a heavy curtain of royal purple.

Here all the courtiers knelt, bending over to touch the floor with their foreheads, in token of homage to The Great King. The officer now bade Hippias do likewise; and when the Athenian raised his head, after reluctantly going through this performance, he saw that the curtain had been quietly pulled aside.

On a beautiful throne of ivory and gold, all overshadowed by a golden vine bearing clusters of jeweled grapes, sat the Persian king. He was clad in superbly embroidered robes, wore a diamond crown or tiara, held a scepter of pure gold, and was surrounded by his officers, who were almost as richly dressed as he.

As the Athenians were plain people, Hippias had never seen such a sight before, and stared at the garments, which were far handsomer than those which the Greek gods were given to wear.

Invited to speak freely and make his errand known, Hippias now told Darius that he had come to ask his aid against the revolted Athenians. Darius listened politely to all he had to say, and then sent him away, graciously promising to think the matter over, and giving orders that Hippias should be royally entertained in the mean while.

Among Darius' numerous slaves, most of whom were captives of war, there was a learned Greek doctor called Dem-o-ce´des. This man, hoping soon to recover his freedom by paying a sum of money, was very careful to hide his name, and not to tell any one how much he knew.

It happened, however, that the king hurt his foot; and after the Persian doctors had all vainly tried to cure him, he sent for Democedes, saying that he would put him to death if he did not speedily help him.

Thus forced to use his knowledge, Democedes did all he could for the king, and treated the wound so skillfully that the monarch was soon cured. The king, who had found out from the other captives that the man was a doctor, now named him court physician, and even had him attend his wives.

One of these women was A-tos´sa, the favorite queen; and when she became ill, Democedes was fortunate enough to save her life. The king was so delighted with this cure, that he bade Democedes choose any reward he pleased except his freedom.

Democedes, after a few moments' thought, asked permission to visit his native land once more; and Darius let him go under the escort of fifteen officers, who had orders not to lose sight of the doctor for a moment, to bring him back by force if necessary, and to spy out the land.

In spite of the constant watching of these fifteen men, Democedes managed to escape while they were in Greece, and hid so well that they were never able to find him. They were therefore obliged to go home without him; and as soon as they arrived in Persia, they reported to Darius all they had done on the way.

The Great King questioned them very closely about all they had seen; and his curiosity was so excited by what they told him, that he made up his mind to conquer Greece and add it to his kingdom.

He therefore sent for Hippias again, told him that he was ready to help him, and gave orders to collect one of the largest armies that had ever been seen. With this army he hoped not only to take the whole country, but also to get back the runaway doctor, Democedes, who in the mean while was living peacefully in Greece, where he had married a daughter of the famous strong man, Milo of Croton.

XLII. DESTRUCTION OF THE PERSIAN HOST.

The Persian preparations for war were hastened by news that all the Ionian cities had rebelled. These were, as you remember, Greek colonies founded on the coast of Asia Minor. They had little by little fallen into the hands of the Persians; but, as they hated to submit to foreign rule, they had long planned a revolt.

The Athenians, who knew that the Persians were talking of coming over to conquer them, now offered to help the Ionians, and sent some troops over to Asia Minor. These joined the rebels, and together they managed to surprise and burn to the ground the rich city of Sar´dis, which belonged to Darius.

A messenger was sent in hot haste to bear these tidings to The Great King; and when he heard them, he was very angry indeed. In his wrath, he said that he would punish both rebels and Athenians, and immediately sent his army into Ionia.

The first part of his vow was easily kept, for his troops soon defeated the Ionian army, and forced the rebels to obey him once more. When Darius heard this, he was very much pleased; and then, sending for his bow, he shot an arrow in the direction of Athens, to show that the punishment of the Athenians would be his next care.

As he was afraid of forgetting these enemies in the pressure of other business, he gave orders that a slave should appear before him every day while he sat at dinner, and solemnly say, "Master, remember the Athenians!"

When the preparations for this distant war were ended, the Persian army set out for Greece. In order to reach that country, it had to march a long way through the northern part of Asia Minor, cross a narrow strait called the Hel´les-pont, and pass along the coast of the Ægean Sea, through Thrace and Scyth´i-a.

In these countries the Persian army met the fierce and warlike Scyth´i-ans mounted on their fleet-footed horses, and was nearly cut to pieces. The Persians were so frightened by the attack of these foes, that they refused to go any farther, and even beat a hasty retreat.

The Persian fleet in the mean while had sailed along bravely. It soon came to the promontory formed by Mount A´thos, a tall mountain which sometimes casts a shadow eighty miles long over the sea. Here a terrible tempest overtook the fleet, and the waves rose so high that six hundred vessels were dashed to pieces.

All the rest of the Persian vessels were so damaged by the storm, that it was soon decided that they had better return home. The soldiers of The Great King were of course greatly discouraged by these misfortunes; but Darius was more than ever determined to conquer Greece, and at once began to gather a second army and to build a second fleet.

XLIII. THE ADVANCE OF THE SECOND HOST.

Darius was very busy preparing this other army to march against Greece. While the men were being drilled, he sent two messengers to the Greek towns and islands, bidding them surrender and give him earth and water.

By demanding "earth and water," Darius meant that he wanted them to recognize him as their king, and as master of all their lands and vessels. The inhabitants of many of the islands and towns were so frightened by the messages sent by The Great King, that they humbly yielded; but when the messengers came to Sparta and Athens, they met with a different reception.

In both cities the people proudly replied that they were their own masters, and would not yield to the demands of the Persian king. Then, angered by the insolent command to give earth and water, the Spartans entirely forgot that the life of an ambassador is sacred. In their rage, they seized the Persians, flung one into a pit and the other into a well, and told them to take all the earth and water they wanted.

This conduct made Darius all the more angry, and he hastened his preparations as much as he could. He was so active that in a short time he was able to start out again, with an army of a hundred and twenty thousand men.

The generals of this force were Da´tis and Ar-ta-pher´-nes, who were guided and advised by the traitor Hippias. The fleet was to land the army on the plain of Mar´a-thon, close by the sea, and only one day's journey from Athens.

When the Athenians heard that the Persians were coming, they immediately decided to ask the Spartans, who were now their allies, to come to their aid, and help them drive back the enemy. As there was no time to lose, they chose as their messenger a fleet-footed Athenian, who made the journey of a hundred and fifty miles in a few hours, running every step of the way, and only seldom pausing to rest.

Themistocles.

The Spartans listened breathlessly to his tidings, and promised that they would help the Athenians; but they added, that they would not be able to start until the moon was full, for they thought that they would be beaten unless they set out at a certain time.

The Persians in the mean while were advancing rapidly, so the Athenians started out to meet them with no other help than that of their neighbors the Pla-tæ´ans. The whole Greek force numbered only ten thousand men, and was under the command of the ten Athenian generals who were each entitled to the leadership for a day in turn.

Among these ten Athenian generals were three remarkable men,—Mil-ti´a-des, Ar-is-ti´des, and The-mis´to-cles. They consulted together, hoping to find a plan by which their small army could successfully oppose the Persian host, which was twelve times greater.

At last Miltiades proposed a plan which might succeed, provided there was but one chief, and all obeyed him well.

Aristides, who was not only a good man, but also remarkably just and wise, at once saw the importance of such a plan, and offered to give up his day's command, and to carry out his friend's orders just as if he were nothing but a common soldier.

The other generals, not wishing to appear less generous than he, also gave up their command to Miltiades, who thus found himself general in chief of the Athenian and Platæan armies. So he speedily made his preparations, and drew up his small force on the plain of Marathon, between the mountains and the sea.

XLIV. THE BATTLE OF MARATHON.

The Greek army seemed so very small beside the huge host of invaders, that the Persians felt perfectly sure that it would surrender as soon as the fight began. Imagine their surprise, therefore, when the Greeks, instead of waiting for them, gave the signal for battle, and rushed furiously upon them.

The daring and force of the Greek attack so confused the Persians, that they began to give way. This encouraged the Greeks still further, and they fought with such bravery that soon the army of The Great King was completely routed.

Hippias, fighting at the head of the Persian army, was one of the first to die; and when the Persians saw their companions falling around them like ripe grain under the mower's scythe, they were seized with terror, rushed toward the sea, and embarked in their vessels in great haste.

The Athenians followed the enemy closely, killing all they could reach, and trying to prevent them from embarking and so escaping their wrath. One Greek soldier even rushed down into the waves, and held a Persian vessel which was about to push off.

The Persians, anxious to escape, struck at him, and chopped off his hand; but the Greek, without hesitating a moment, grasped the boat with his other hand, and held it fast. In their hurry to get away, the Persians struck off that hand too; but the dauntless hero caught and held the boat with his strong teeth, and died beneath the repeated blows of the enemy without having once let go. Thanks to him, not one of those enemies escaped.

The victory was a glorious one. The whole Persian force had been routed by a mere handful of men; and the Athenians were so proud of their victory, that they longed to have their fellow-citizens rejoice with them.

One of the soldiers, who had fought bravely all day, and who was covered with blood, said he would carry the glad news, and, without waiting a moment, he started off at a run.

Such was his haste to reassure the Athenians, that he ran at his utmost speed, and reached the city in a few hours. He was so exhausted, however, that he had barely time to gasp out, "Rejoice, we have conquered!" before he sank down in the middle of the market place, dead.

The Greeks, having no more foes to kill, next began to rob the tents, where they found so much booty that each man became quite rich. Then they gathered up their dead, and buried them honorably on the battlefield, at a spot where they afterward erected ten small columns bearing the names of all who had lost their lives in the conflict.

Just as all was over, the Spartan force came rushing up, ready to give their promised aid. They were so sorry not to have had a chance to fight also, and to have missed a share in the glory, that they vowed they would never again allow any superstition to prevent their striking a blow for their native land whenever the necessity arose.

Miltiades, instead of permitting his weary soldiers to camp on the battlefield, and celebrate their victory by a grand feast, next ordered them to march on to the city, so as to defend it in case the

Persian fleet came to attack it.

The troops had scarcely arrived in town and taken up their post there, when the Persian vessels came in; but when the soldiers attempted to land, and saw the same men ready to meet them, they were so dismayed that they beat a hasty retreat without striking another blow.

XLV. MILTIADES' DISGRACE.

The victory of Marathon was a great triumph for the Athenians; and Miltiades, who had so successfully led them, was loaded with honors. His portrait was painted by the best artist of the day, and it was placed in one of the porticos of Athens, where every one could see it.

At his request, the main part of the booty was given to the gods, for the Greeks believed that it was owing to divine favor that they had conquered their enemies. The brazen arms and shields which they had taken from the ten thousand Persians killed were therefore melted, and formed into an immense statue of Athene, which was placed on the Acropolis, on a pedestal so high that the glittering lance which the goddess held could be seen far out at sea when the sunbeams struck its point.

The Athenians vented their triumph and delight in song and dance, in plays and works of art of all kinds; for they wished to commemorate the glorious victory which had cost them only a hundred and ninety men, while the enemy had lost ten thousand.

One of their choicest art treasures was made by Phidias, the greatest sculptor the world has ever known, out of a beautiful block of marble which Darius had brought from Persia. The Great King had intended to set it up in Athens as a monument of his victory over the Greeks. It was used instead to record his defeat; and when finished, the statue represented Nem´e-sis, the goddess of retribution, whose place it was to punish the proud and insolent, and to make them repent of their sins.

Miltiades was, as we have seen, the idol of the Athenian people after his victory at Marathon. Unfortunately, however, they were inclined to be fickle; and when they saw that Miltiades occupied such a high rank, many began to envy him.

Themistocles was particularly jealous of the great honors that his friend had won. His friends soon noticed his gloomy, discontented looks; and when they inquired what caused them, Themistocles said it was because the thought of the trophies of Miltiades would not let him sleep. Some time after, when he saw that Miltiades was beginning to misuse his power, he openly showed his dislike.

Not very far from Athens, out in the Ægean Sea, was the Island of Pa´ros. The people living there were enemies of Miltiades; and he, being sole head of the fleet, led it thither to avenge his personal wrongs.

The expedition failed, however; and Miltiades came back to Athens, where Themistocles and the indignant citizens accused him of betraying his trust, tried him, and convicted him of treason.

Had they not remembered the service that he had rendered his country in defeating the Persians at Marathon, they would surely have condemned him to death. As it was, the jury merely sentenced him to pay a heavy fine, saying that he should remain in prison until it was paid.

Miltiades was not rich enough to raise this large sum of money, so he died in prison. His son Ci´mon went to claim his body, so that he might bury it properly; but the hard-hearted judges refused to let him have it until he had paid his father's debt.

Thus forced to turn away without his father's corpse, Cimon visited his friends, who lent him the necessary money. Miltiades, who had been the idol of the people, was now buried hurriedly and in secret, because the ungrateful Athenians had forgotten all the good he had done them, and remembered only his faults.

XLVI. ARISTIDES THE JUST.

The Athenians were very happy, because they thought, that, having once defeated the Persians, they need fear them no more. They were greatly mistaken, however. The Great King had twice seen his preparations come to naught and his plans ruined, but he was not yet ready to give up the hope of conquering Greece.

On the contrary, he solemnly swore that he would return with a greater army than ever, and make himself master of the proud city which had defied him. These plans were suspected by Themistocles, who therefore urged the Athenians to strengthen their navy, so that they might be ready for war when it came.

Aristides, the other general, was of the opinion that it was useless to build any more ships, but that the Athenians should increase their land forces. As each general had a large party, many quarrels soon arose. It became clear before long, that, unless one of the two leaders left the town, there would be an outbreak of civil war.

All the Athenians, therefore, gathered together in the market place, where they were to vote for or against the banishment of one of the leaders. Of course, on this great occasion, all the workmen left their labors, and even the farmers came in from the fields.

Aristides was walking about among the voters, when a farmer stopped him. The man did not know who he was, but begged him to write his vote down on the shell, for he had never even learned to read.

"What name shall I write?" questioned Aristides.

"Oh, put down 'Aristides,'" answered the farmer.

"Why do you want him sent away? Has he ever done you any harm?" asked Aristides.

"No," said the man, "but I'm tired of hearing him called the Just."

Without saying another word, Aristides calmly wrote his own name on the shell. When the votes were counted, they found six thousand against him: so Aristides the Just was forced to leave his native city, and go away into exile.

This was a second example of Athenian ingratitude; for Aristides had never done anything wrong, but had, on the contrary, done all he could to help his country. His enemies, however, were the men who were neither honest nor just, and who felt that his virtues were a constant rebuke to them; and this was the very reason why they were so anxious to get him out of the city.

XLVII. TWO NOBLE SPARTAN YOUTHS.

Darius was in the midst of his preparations for a third expedition to Greece, when all his plans were cut short by death. His son and successor, Xerx´es I., now became King of Persia in his stead.

The new monarch was not inclined to renew the struggle with the Greeks; but his courtiers and the exiled Greeks who dwelt in his palace so persistently urged him to do it, that he finally consented. Orders were then sent throughout the kingdom to get ready for war, and Xerxes said that he would lead the army himself.

During eight years the constant drilling of troops, manufacture of arms, collecting of provisions, and construction of roads, were kept up all through Asia. A mighty fleet lay at anchor, and the king was almost ready to start. Rumors of these great preparations had, of course, come to the ears of the Greeks. All hearts were filled with trouble and fear; for the coming army was far larger than the one the Athenians had defeated at Marathon, and they could not expect to be so fortunate again.

When the Spartans saw the terror of the people, they regretted having angered the king by killing the Persian messengers, and wondered what they could do to disarm his wrath. Two young men, Bu´lis and Sper´thi-as, then nobly resolved to offer their lives in exchange for those that had been taken.

They therefore set out for Persia, and, having obtained permission to enter the palace, appeared before the king. Here the courtiers bade them fall down before the monarch, and do homage to him, as they saw the others do. But the proud young men refused to do so, saying that such honor could be shown only to their gods, and that it was not the custom of their country to humble themselves thus. Xerxes, to the surprise of his courtiers did not at all resent their refusal to fall down before him, but kindly bade them make their errand known.

Thus invited to speak, one of them replied, "King of Persia, some years ago our people killed two of your father's messengers. It was wrong to touch an ambassador, we know. You are about to visit our country to seek revenge for this crime. Desist, O king! for we have come hither, my friend and I, to offer our lives in exchange for those our people have taken. Here we are! Do with us as you will."

Xerxes was filled with admiration when he heard this speech, and saw the handsome youths standing quietly before him, ready to die to atone for their country's wrong. Instead of accepting their offer, he loaded them with rich gifts, and sent them home unharmed, telling them he would not injure the innocent, for he was more just than the Lac-e-dæ-mo´ni-ans.

But a few months later, when his preparations were complete, Xerxes set out with an army which is said to have numbered more than two million fighting men. As they were attended by slaves and servants of all kinds, some of the old historians say that ten millions of human beings were included in this mighty host.

XLVIII. THE GREAT ARMY.

Xerxes' army marched in various sections across Asia Minor, and all the forces came together at the Hellespont. Here the king had ordered the building of two great bridges,—one for the troops, and the other for the immense train of baggage which followed him.

These bridges were no sooner finished than a rising storm entirely destroyed them. When Xerxes heard of the disaster, he not only condemned the unlucky engineers to death, but also had the waves flogged with whips, and ordered chains flung across the strait, to show that he considered the sea an unruly slave, who should be taught to obey his master.

Then, undaunted by his misfortune, the King of Persia gave orders for the building of new bridges; and when they were finished, he reviewed his army from the top of a neighboring mountain.

The sight must have been grand indeed, and the courtiers standing around were greatly surprised when they saw their master suddenly burst into tears. When asked the cause of his sorrow, Xerxes answered, "See that mighty host spread out as far as eye can reach! I weep at the thought that a hundred years hence there will be nothing left of it except, perhaps, a handful of dust and a few moldering bones!"

The king was soon comforted, however, and crossed the bridge first, attended by his bodyguard of picked soldiers, who were called the Immortals because they had never suffered defeat. All the army followed him, and during seven days and nights the bridge resounded with the steady tramp of the armed host; but, even when the rear guard had passed over the Hellespont, there were still so many slaves and baggage wagons, that it took them a whole month to file past.

That was a procession such as has never again been seen. You can imagine what a sight it was for all the boys and girls who lived near enough to the Hellespont to see this mighty parade, which continued night and day.

They saw not only the sacred chariot drawn by eight white horses, the glittering array of the Immortals, the burnished helmets and arms of the foot soldiers, and the silken canopies and tents over the grandees, but also countless chariots drawn by four horses, and provided on either side with sharp scythes, which were intended to mow down the enemy like ripe grain.

Crossing the Hellespont.

Besides these strange mowing machines, there were many other engines of war, which were all made to strike terror into the hearts of the Greeks, and to subdue completely the proud people who had so sorely defeated Darius' troops at Marathon.

To prevent his fleet from being wrecked as his father's was, Xerxes had given orders to dig a great canal across the isthmus that connected Mount Athos with the mainland; and through this the vessels sailed past the promontory in safety.

XLIX. PREPARATIONS FOR DEFENSE.

The news of Xerxes' crossing of the Hellespont, and of his approach to conquer Greece, soon reached Athens, where it filled all hearts with fear. The people then remembered Miltiades, and bitterly regretted his death, and their ingratitude, which had been its real cause.

As the mighty general who had already once delivered them was dead, they tried to think who could best replace him, and decided to recall Aristides the Just from his undeserved exile. Aristides generously forgave his fellow-citizens for all the harm they had done him, and he and Themistocles began to do all in their power to insure the safety of Athens.

Swift runners were dispatched in every direction with messages urging all the Greek cities to unite for the good of the country by sending as many brave men as possible to check the Persian army, and to try to hinder it from really entering Greece.

Themistocles was the most active in this attempt to induce the Greek cities to join forces, and it was he who planned a great council, or meeting, at Corinth, in 481 B.C. There it soon became evident that the cities were too jealous of each other to unite as they should.

Many of them promised help, which they never sent; others vowed they would neither send troops nor furnish aid of any kind, unless *their* generals had supreme command; and even the oracles gave vague and discouraging answers, when consulted as usual.

In spite of all these drawbacks, Themistocles managed to get a few allies; and, in order to induce the Spartans to lend their aid, he promised them the command not only of the army, but also of the fleet.

He next persuaded them that it would be wisest to send an armed force into Thessaly, so as to defend the narrow pass of Thermopylæ, which was the only road by which the Persians could enter Greece. This natural causeway, as we have seen, lay between the mountains and the sea; and, because there were springs of warm water here, it was generally known as Thermopylæ, which is the Greek for "Hot Gateway."

Under the guidance of Le-on´i-das, one of the Spartan kings, three hundred Lacedæmonian soldiers and six thousand allies marched thither, and undertook to guard the pass. This was a very small army; but it was impossible to get more soldiers at the time, as all the Greeks were more anxious to attend the Olympic games, which were just then being celebrated, than to defend their country and homes.

Many of them said they were afraid the gods would be angry if they did not keep the feast as usual, and declared that it was against the law to bear arms or make war during that time. This was perfectly true; but Xerxes did not care at all for the Greek gods, and the country would have been defenseless had it not been for Leonidas and his handful of men.

While this little army traveled northwards, the rest of the people thronged to Olympia, promising to come and fight as soon as the games were ended, and they could again bear arms without offending the gods.

The Persian fleet, as you have seen, had passed behind Mount Athos, instead of rounding it as before, and Xerxes intended landing part of his army just below Thermopylæ. Unfortunately for him, however, the four hundred vessels bearing his troops were wrecked by a sudden storm.

Another fleet was immediately prepared; but, before it was ready, the Olympic games came to an end, and the Greeks, flying to arms as they had promised, hastily embarked upon their own vessels, and came and took up their position at Ar-te-mis´ium, to hinder the advance of the Persian fleet.

L. LEONIDAS AT THERMOPYLÆ

The Persian army had come to the Pass of Thermopylæ; and Xerxes, seeing that it was guarded by only a few men, sent them a haughty message, bidding them surrender their arms.

Instead of seeing a meek compliance with this request, as they expected, the Persian heralds were amazed to hear Leonidas reply with true laconic brevity, "Come and take them!"

The Spartan king, however, had quickly seen that it would be impossible for him to do much more than stop for a while the advance of this mighty host. As a Spartan never drew back, he made up his mind to die on the field of battle, and bade his warriors comb their hair, don their choicest armor, and dress themselves in their richest attire, as was the custom when some great danger threatened them and they expected to die.

The Persians, seeing this, were greatly surprised, and advanced confidently, for they fancied that men who took so much trouble to curl and perfume their hair would not be hard to conquer. They soon found out their mistake.

As they advanced, the archers shot a volley of arrows, and in such numbers that they fairly darkened the sun. One of the allies, seeing this, ran to warn Leonidas; but he received the startling news with great coolness, and merely said, "Very well; then we can fight in the shade."

When Xerxes saw that the Greeks would not yield without striking a blow, he gave orders for the battle tobegin. The Persians pressed forward, under the eye of their king, who sat high up on the rocks to see them conquer; but, to his surprise, they were driven back by that mere handful of men.

Again and again they tried to force the pass, but all their attempts proved vain. The Persian soldiers, amazed at the courage of the Greeks, were filled with superstitious fears, and began to refuse to advance, except when driven onward under the stinging blows of the lash.

The king was furious to see their close ranks give way time after time, and finally ordered his own Immortals to march on and scatter the army, which, although so small, was keeping millions of men at bay. He expected that everything would of course give way at the very first charge of these troops.

Imagine his wrath, therefore, when he saw the Immortals also retreat, after many useless efforts to drive away the enemy. The Persians did not know what to do. They could not advance, and were ashamed to retreat.

LI. DEATH OF LEONIDAS.

While the Persians were hesitating thus, a Greek shepherd, Eph-i-al´tes, stole into their camp, and, vile traitor that he was, offered to show them another way to get into Greece, if they would pay him well. This man was led into the tent of a Persian general, where he explained that he could easily lead a troop of Persians over the mountains.

By a goat path known to the Greeks only, it was possible not only to cross the mountains, but also to come down upon the small Greek force guarding the Pass of Thermopylæ.

His offer as guide was accepted. Ephialtes, true to his promise, if not to his country, led the Persian Immortals along this narrow way. Leonidas, who could not imagine that any one of the Greeks would be base enough to sell his country and honor for gold, had placed only a few of the allies at this spot.

The Immortals followed Ephialtes, easily cut these few men down, and came unperceived behind the Spartan troops. It was only when he heard the tramp of horses behind him and on the mountain above him, that Leonidas found out that he had been betrayed.

Hastily calling his allies, he gave them permission to save themselves by flight, declaring, however, that he and his companions would never leave their post, and that, since they could not conquer, they were ready to die.

Some of the allies took advantage of this permission to escape, but seven hundred Thes´pi-ans nobly chose to remain with the Spartans. With the courage of despair, these men now fought against the Persians before and behind them, selling their lives as dearly as possible. In spite of the odds against them, they refused to surrender, and finally fell, one after another, on the spot which they had undertaken to guard.

A Fighting Persian.

Their bodies, which were found almost in a heap,—for they had scorned to fly,—were honorably buried in a single mound, over which rose a monument with this modest inscription,—

"Go, passer-by, at Sparta tell,
Obedient to her law we fell."

The Persians had forced their way into Greece. Nothing could check their further advance, so the mighty army swept southward. The first place of note on their way to Athens was Delphi, the site of the sacred temple, where great treasures were stored.

The Greeks knew that the Persians did not worship the same gods, and feared that they might rob the temple: so they now eagerly questioned the oracle, to find out whether they should not all assemble there in its defense.

To their surprise, the oracle proudly replied, "The gods will take care of their own," and bade them rather use their strength to defend their own homes.

The Persians marched into the rocky gorge leading to the temple at Delphi, but just as they were entering the valley a terrible thunderstorm broke forth. The darkness became so great that the soldiers lost their way. The rocks rolled and crashed down upon them; and the soldiers, filled with dread, beat a hasty retreat, and never again dared venture into this valley.

In the mean while the Greek fleet at Artemisium had held the Persian vessels at bay, until news was brought of the death of Leonidas, and the passage of Thermopylæ. Then the Greeks sailed as fast as they could toward Athens, knowing that they would be needed there to defend the city.

The various allies, sure that it would be quite useless to try to defend the northern part of Greece any longer, retreated into the Peloponnesus, and, hoping to prevent the Persians from entering there, hastily began to build a huge wall all across the Isthmus of Corinth, which is only about five miles wide.

LII. THE BURNING OF ATHENS.

As all their allies were trying only to defend the Peloponnesus, the Athenians were left entirely alone. Many of their friends advised them to abandon their city, and follow the other Greeks southward, leaving all Attica a prey to the foe.

This the Athenians did not wish to do, so they sent in haste to Delphi, to inquire of the oracle whether they had better retreat, or attempt to defend their city. As was generally the case, the oracle did not give a plain answer, but merely said, "The wooden walls will defend you and your children."

When this answer was brought to Athens, no one could tell exactly what it meant. Some of the citizens fancied that the oracle was advising them to retreat behind the ancient wooden stockade on the Acropolis, but Themistocles insisted that by "wooden walls" the oracle meant their ships.

He finally persuaded the Athenians to believe him. All the old men, women, and children were hastily brought on board the ships, and carried to the Peloponnesus, where they were welcomed by their friends. Then the men embarked in their turn, and the fleet sailed off to the Bay of Sal'a-mis, where it awaited a good chance to fight.

The Persians swept down into Attica, and entered the deserted city of Athens. Here they gazed in wonder at all they saw, and, after robbing the houses, set fire to the town, and burned down all the most beautiful buildings.

The Persians were so delighted at having attained their purpose, and reduced the proud city to ashes, that they sent messengers to bear the glad tidings to the Persian capital. Here the people became almost wild with joy, and the whole city rang with their cries of triumph for many a day.

As you will remember, Themistocles had allowed the Spartans to command both the army and the navy. It was therefore a Spartan king, Eu-ry-bi'a-des, who was head of the fleet at Salamis. He was a careful man, and was not at all in favor of attacking the Persians.

Themistocles, on the contrary, felt sure that an immediate attack, being unexpected, would prove successful,and therefore loudly insisted upon it. His persistency in urging it finally made Eurybiades so angry that he exclaimed, "Those who begin the race before the signal is given are publicly scourged!"

Themistocles, however, would not allow even this remark to annoy him, and calmly answered, "Very true, but laggards never win a crown!" The reply, which Eurybiades thought was meant for an insult, so enraged him that he raised his staff to strike the bold speaker. At this, the brave Athenian neither drew back nor flew into a passion: he only cried, "Strike if you will, but hear me!"

Once more Themistocles explained his reasons for urging an immediate attack; and his plans were so good, that Eurybiades, who could but admire his courage, finally yielded, and gave orders to prepare for battle.

LIII. THE BATTLES OF SALAMIS AND PLATÆA.

The fleets soon came face to face; and Xerxes took up his post on a mountain, where he sat in state upon a hastily built throne to see his vessels destroy the enemy. He had made very clever plans, and, as his fleet was far larger than that of the Greeks, he had no doubt that he would succeed in defeating them.

His plans, however, had been found out by Aristides, who was in the Island of Ægina; and this noble man rowed over to the fleet, at the risk of being caught by the enemy, to warn his fellow-citizens of their danger.

He first spoke to Themistocles, saying, "Rivals we have always been; let us now set all other rivalry aside, and only strive which can best serve his native country."

Themistocles agreed to this proposal, and managed affairs so wisely and bravely that the Greeks won a great victory. When they came home in triumph with much spoil, the women received them with cries of joy, and strewed flowers under their feet.

From his high position, Xerxes saw his fleet cut to pieces; and he was so discouraged by this check, that he hastened back to Persia, leaving his brother-in-law Mar-do'ni-us with an army of three hundred thousand men to finish the conquest of Greece.

The Greeks were so happy over their naval victory at Salamis, that they all flew to arms once more; and Pau-sa'ni-as, the Spartan king, the successor of Leonidas, was soon able to lead a large army against Mardonius.

The two forces met at Pla-tæ'a, and again the Greeks won, although fighting against foes who greatly outnumbered them. Strange to relate, while Pausanias was winning one battle at Platæa, the other Spartan king, Eurybiades, defeated a new Persian fleet at Myc'a-le.

These two victories finished the rout of the greatest army ever seen. Mardonius fled with the remnant of his host, leaving his tents, baggage, and slaves to the Greeks, who thus got much booty.

We are told that the Spartans, entering the Persian camp, were greatly amazed at the luxury of the tents. Pausanias stopped in the one that had been occupied by Mardonius, and bade the slaves prepare a meal such as they had been wont to lay before their master.

Return of the Victorious Greeks.

Then, calling his own Helots, he gave orders for his usual supper. When both meals were ready, they made the greatest contrast. The Persian tent was all decked with costly hangings, the table was spread with many kinds of rich food served in dishes of solid gold, and soft couches were spread for the guests.

The Spartan supper, on the contrary, was of the plainest description, and was served in ordinary earthenware. Pausanias called his officers and men, and, after pointing out the difference between the Spartan and the Persian style of living, he showed how much he liked plain food by eating his usual supper.

To reward Pausanias for his bravery and for defeating the enemy, the Greeks gave him a part of all that was best in the spoil. Next they set aside one tenth of it for Apollo, and sent it to his priests at Delphi as a token of gratitude for the favor of the god.

To show that they were grateful also to Zeus and Poseidon,—the gods who, they thought, had helped them to win their battles by land and by sea,—they sent statues to Olympia and Corinth; and they erected a temple in honor of Athene, the goddess of defensive war, on the battlefield of Platæa.

LIV. THE REBUILDING OF ATHENS.

The Persians had been driven out of Greece, and the war with them was now carried on in Asia Minor instead of nearer home. The Greek army wonmany battles here also, and even managed to free the city of Miletus from the Persian yoke.

These triumphs encouraged all the Ionian cities, and they soon formed a league with the other Greeks, promising to help them against the Persians should the war ever be renewed. As soon as this alliance was made, the Greek fleet returned home, bringing back to Athens as a trophy the chains with which Xerxes had pretended to bind the rebellious sea.

In the mean while the Athenians, who had taken refuge on the Peloponnesus, had returned to their native city, where, alas! they found their houses and temples in ruins. The desolation was great; yet the people were so thankful to return, that they prepared to rebuild the town.

They were greatly encouraged in this purpose by an event which seemed to them a good omen. Near the temple of the patron goddess of Athens stood a sacred olive tree, supposed to have been created by her at the time when the city received her name.

This place had been burned by the invaders, and the returning Athenians sorrowfully gazed upon the blackened trunk of the sacred tree. Imagine their delight, therefore, when a new shoot suddenly sprang up from the ashes, and put forth leaves with marvelous speed.

The people all cried that the goddess had sent them this sign of her continued favor to encourage them to rebuild the city, and they worked with such energy that they were soon provided with new homes.

As soon as the Athenians had secured shelter for their families, they began to restore the mighty walls which had been the pride of their city. When the Spartans heard of this, they jealously objected, for they were afraid that Athens would become more powerful than Sparta.

Of course, they did not want to own that they were influenced by so mean a feeling as jealousy, so they tried to find a pretext to hinder the work. This was soon found, and Spartan messengers came and told the Athenians that they should not fortify the town, lest it should fall again into the hands of the enemy, and serve them as a stronghold.

Themistocles suspected the real cause of these objections, and made up his mind to use all his talents to help his fellow-citizens. He therefore secretly assembled the most able men, and told them to go on with the work as fast as possible, while he went to Sparta to talk over the matter with the Lacedæmonians.

When he arrived at Sparta, he artfully prolonged the discussions until the walls were built high enough to be defended. Of course, there was now nothing to be done; but the Spartans were very angry, and waited anxiously for an opportunity to punish the Athenians. This came after a time, as you will see in the following chapters.

LV. DEATH OF PAUSANIAS.

Pausanias, the Spartan king, was very proud of the great victory he had won over the Persians at Platæa, and of the praise and booty he had received. He was so proud of it, that he soon became unbearable, and even wanted to become ruler of all Greece.

Although he had at first pretended to despise the luxury which he had seen in the tent of Mardonius, he soon began to put on the Persian dress and to copy their manners, and demanded much homage from his subjects. This greatly displeased the simple Greeks, and he soon saw that they would not help him to become sole king.

In his ambition to rule alone, he entirely forgot all that was right, and, turning traitor, secretly offered to help the Persians if they would promise to make him king over all Greece.

This base plot was found out by the ephors, the officers whose duty it was to watch the kings, and they ordered his own guards to seize him. Before this order could be carried out, however, Pausanias fled, and took refuge in a neighboring temple, where, of course, no one could lay violent hands upon him.

As the ephors feared he might even yet escape to Persia, and carry out his wicked plans, they ordered that the doors and windows of the temple should all be walled up.

It is said that as soon as this command had been given, Pausanias' mother brought the first stone, saying she preferred that her son should die, rather than live to be a traitor.

Thus walled in, Pausanias slowly starved to death, and the barriers were torn down only just in time to allow him to be carried out, and breathe his last in the open air. The Spartans would not let him die in the temple, because they thought his dying breath would offend the gods.

As Themistocles had been a great friend of Pausanias, he was accused of sharing his plans. The Athenians therefore rose up against him in anger, ostracized him, and drove him out of the country to end his life in exile.

After wandering aimlessly about for some time, Themistocles finally went to the court of Ar-tax-erx´es, the son and successor of Xerxes.

The Persian monarch, we are told, welcomed him warmly, gave him a Persian wife, and set aside three cities to supply him with bread, meat, and wine. Themistocles soon grew very rich, and lived on the fat of the land; and a traveler said that he once exclaimed, "How much we should have lost, my children and I, had we not been ruined by the Athenians!"

Artaxerxes, having thus provided for all Themistocles' wants, and helped him to pile up riches, fancied that his gratitude would lead him to perform any service the king might ask. He therefore sent for Themistocles one day, and bade him lead a Persian army against the Greeks.

But, although Themistocles had been exiled from his country, he had not fallen low enough to turn traitor. He proudly refused to fight; and it is said that he preferred to commit suicide, rather than injure the people he had once loved so dearly.

LVI. CIMON IMPROVES ATHENS.

As soon as Themistocles had been banished from Athens, Aristides again became the chief man of the city, and he was also made the head and leader of the allies. He was so upright and just that all were ready to honor and obey him, and they gladly let him take charge of the money of the state.

In reward for his services, the Athenians offered him a large salary and many rich gifts; but he refused them all, saying that he needed nothing, and could afford to serve his country without pay.

He therefore went on seeing to all the public affairs until his death, when it was found that he was so poor that there was not enough money left to pay for his funeral. The Athenians, touched by his virtues, gave him a public burial, held his name in great honor, and often regretted that they had once been so ungrateful as to banish their greatest citizen, Aristides the Just.

As Aristides had watched carefully over the money of the allied states, and had ruled the Athenians very wisely, it is no wonder that Athens had little by little risen above Sparta, which had occupied the first place ever since the battle of Thermopylæ.

The Athenians, as long as Aristides lived, showed themselves just and liberal; but as soon as he was dead, they began to treat their former allies unkindly. The money which all the Greek states furnished was now no longer used to strengthen the army and navy, as first agreed, but was lavishly spent to beautify the city.

Now, while it was a good thing to make their town as fine as possible, it was certainly wrong to use the money of others for this purpose, and the Athenians were soon punished for their dishonesty.

Cimon, the son of Miltiades, was made the head of the army, and won several victories over the Persians in Asia Minor. When he returned to Athens, he brought back a great deal of spoil, and generously gave up all his share to improve the city and strengthen the walls.

The Theseum.

It is said that Cimon also enlarged the beautiful gardens of the A-cad´e-my; and the citizens, by wandering up and down the shady walks, showed that they liked this as well as the Lyceum, which, you will remember, Pisistratus had given them.

They also went in crowds to these gardens to hear the philosophers, who taught in the cool porticoes or stone piazzas built all around them, and there they learned many good things.

Cimon showed his patriotism in still another way by persuading the people that the remains of

Theseus, their ancient king, should rest in the city. Theseus' bones were therefore brought from Scyros, the island where he had been killed so treacherously, and were buried near the center of Athens, where the resting-place of this great man was marked by a temple called the The-se'um. A building of this name is still standing in the city; and, although somewhat damaged, it is now used as a museum, and contains a fine statue of Theseus.

LVII. THE EARTHQUAKE.

Cimon, as you have already seen, was very wealthy, and as generous as he was rich. Besides spending so much for the improvement of the city, he always kept an open house. His table was bountifully spread, and he gladly received as guests all who chose to walk into his home.

Whenever he went out, he was followed by servants who carried full purses, and whose duty it was to help all the poor they met. As Cimon knew that many of the most deserving poor would have been ashamed to receive alms, these men found out their wants, and supplied them secretly.

Now, although Cimon was so good and thoughtful, you must not imagine that it was always very easy for him to be so. It seems that when he was a young man he was very idle and lazy, and never thought of anything but his own pleasure.

Aristides the Just noticed how lazy and selfish the young man was, and one day went to see him. After a little talk, Aristides told him seriously that he ought to be ashamed of the life he was living, as it was quite unworthy of a good citizen or of a noble man.

This reproof was so just, that Cimon promised to do better, and tried so hard that he soon became one of the most industrious and unselfish men of his day.

Cimon was not the only rich man in Athens, however; for Per'i-cles, another citizen, was even wealthier than he. As Pericles was shrewd, learned, and very eloquent, he soon gained much influence over his fellow-citizens.

While Cimon was generally seen in the company of men of his own class, and was hence considered the leader of the nobles or aristocrats, Pericles liked to talk with the poorer class, whom he could easily sway by his eloquent speeches, and who soon made him their idol.

Day by day the two parties became more distinct, and soon the Athenians sided either with Pericles or with Cimon in all important matters. The two leaders were at first very good friends, but little by little they drifted apart, and finally they became rivals.

About this time an earthquake brought great misfortunes upon Greece. The whole country shook and swayed, and the effects of the earthquake were so disastrous at Sparta that all the houses and temples were destroyed.

Many of the inhabitants were crushed under the falling stones and timbers, and there were only five houses left standing. The Spartans were in despair; and the Helots, or slaves, who had long been waiting for an opportunity to free themselves, fancied that the right time had come.

They quickly assembled, and decided to kill the Spartans while they were groping about among the ruined dwellings for the remains of their relatives and friends.

The plan would have succeeded had not the king, Ar-chi-da'mus, found it out. Without a moment's delay, he rallied all the able-bodied men, and sent a swift messenger to Athens for aid.

True to their military training, the Spartans dropped everything when the summons reached them; and the Helots came marching along, only to find their former masters drawn up in battle array, and as calm as if no misfortune had happened.

This unexpected resistance so frightened the Helots, that they hastily withdrew into Messenia. Here they easily persuaded the Messenians to join forces with them and declare war against the

Spartans.

In the mean while the swift runner sent by Archidamus had reached Athens, and told about the destruction of the town and the perilous situation of the people. He ended by imploring the Athenians to send immediate aid, lest all the Spartans should perish.

Cimon, who was generous and kind-hearted, immediately cried out that the Athenians could not refuse to help their unhappy neighbors; but Pericles, who, like most of his fellow-citizens, hated the Spartans, advised all his friends to stay quietly at home.

Much discussion took place over this advice. At last, however, Cimon prevailed, and an army was sent to help the Spartans. Owing to the hesitation of the Athenians, this army came late, and they fought with so little spirit that the Lacedæmonians indignantly said that they might just as well have remained at home.

This insult so enraged the Athenians that they went home; and when it became publicly known how the Spartans had treated their army, the people began to murmur against Cimon. In their anger, they forgot all the good he had done them, and, assembling in the market place, they ostracized him.

LVIII. THE AGE OF PERICLES.

As soon as Cimon had been banished, Pericles became sole leader of the Athenians; and as he governed them during a long and prosperous time, this period is generally known as the Age of Pericles.

The Spartans who had so rudely sent away their Athenian allies manfully resolved to help themselves, and set about it so vigorously that they soon brought the Helots back to order, and rebuilt their city. When they had settled themselves comfortably, however, they remembered the lukewarm help which had been given them, and determined to punish the Athenians.

The Persian general was just then planning a new invasion of Greece, so the Athenians found themselvesthreatened with a twofold danger. In their distress they recalled Cimon, who was an excellent general, and implored him to take command of their forces.

Cimon fully justified their confidence, and not only won several victories over the Spartans, but compelled them at last to agree to a truce of five years. This matter settled, he next attacked the Persians, whom he soon defeated by land and by sea.

He then forced Artaxerxes, the Persian king, to swear a solemn oath that he would never again wage war against the Athenians, and forbade the Persian vessels ever to enter the Ægean Sea.

Pericles.

These triumphs won, Cimon died from the wounds he had received during the war. His death, however, was kept secret for a whole month, so that the people would have time to get used to a new leader, and not be afraid to fight without their former general.

While Cimon was thus successfully battling with the enemy abroad, Pericles had managed affairs at home. He urged the Athenians to finish their walls; and by his advice they built also the Long Walls, which joined the city to the Pi-ræ´us, a seaport five miles away.

Pericles also increased the Athenian navy, so that, by the time the five-years' truce was over, he had a fine fleet to use in fighting against the Spartans.

As every victory won by the Athenians had only made Sparta more jealous, the war was renewed, and carried on with great fury on both sides. The Spartans gained the first victories; but, owing to their better navy, the Athenians soon won over all the neighboring cities, and got the upper hand of their foes.

The Acropolis.

They were about to end the war by a last victory at Cor-o-ne′a, when fortune suddenly deserted them, and they were so sorely beaten that they were very glad to agree to a truce and return home.

By the treaty then signed, the Athenians bound themselves to keep the peace during a term of thirty years. In exchange, the Spartans allowed them to retain the cities which they had conquered, and the leadership of one of the confederacies formed by the Greek states, reserving the head of the other for themselves.

During these thirty years of peace, Pericles was very busy, and his efforts were directed for the most part toward the improvement of Athens. By his advice a magnificent temple, the Par′the-non, was built on top of the Acropolis, in honor of Athene.

This temple, one of the wonders of the world, was decorated with beautiful carvings by Phidias, and all the rich Athenians went to see them as soon as they were finished. This sculptor also made a magnificent gold and ivory statue of the goddess, to stand in the midst of the Parthenon. But in spite of all his talent, Phidias had many enemies. After a while they wrongfully accused him of stealing part of the gold intrusted to him. Phidias vainly tried to defend himself; but they would not listen to him, and put him in prison, where he died.

Between the temple of Athene and the city there was a series of steps and beautiful porticoes, decorated with paintings and sculptures, which have never been surpassed.

Many other beautiful buildings were erected under the rule of Pericles; and the beauty and art loving Athenians could soon boast that their city was the finest in the world. Artists from all parts of the country thronged thither in search of work, and all were well received by Pericles.

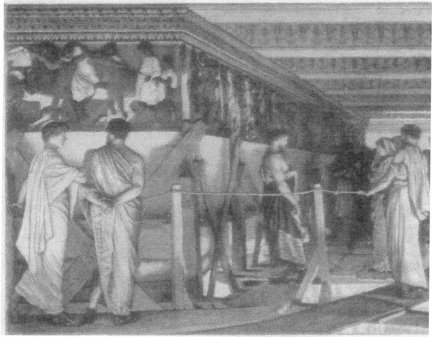

Phidias.

LIX. THE TEACHINGS OF ANAXAGORAS.

As Pericles was a very cultivated man, he liked to meet and talk with the philosophers, and to befriend the artists. He was greatly attached to the sculptor Phidias, and he therefore did all in his power to save him from the envy of his fellow-citizens.

An-ax-ag'o-ras, a philosopher of great renown, was the friend and teacher of Pericles. He, too, won the dislike of the people; and, as they could not accuse him also of stealing, they charged him with publicly teaching that the gods they worshiped were not true gods, and proposed to put him to death for this crime.

Now, Anaxagoras had never heard of the true God, the God whom we worship. He had heard only of Zeus, Athene, and the other gods honored by his people; but he was so wise and so thoughtful that he believed the world could never have been created by such divinities as those.

He observed all he saw very attentively, and shocked the people greatly by saying that the sun was not a god driving in a golden chariot, but a great glowing rock, which, in spite of its seemingly small size, he thought must be about as large as the Peloponnesus.

Of course, this seems very strange to you. But Anaxagoras lived more than two thousand years ago, and since then people have constantly been finding out new things and writing them in books, so it is no wonder that in this matter you are already, perhaps, wiser than he. When you come to study about the sun, you will find that Anaxagoras was partly right, but that, instead of being only as large as the Peloponnesus, the sun is more than a million times larger than the whole earth!

Anaxagoras also tried to explain that the moon was probably very much like the earth, with mountains, plains, and seas. These things, which they could not understand, made the Athenians so angry that they exiled the philosopher, in spite of all Pericles could say.

Anaxagoras went away without making any fuss, and withdrew to a distant city, where he continued his studies as before. Many people regretted his absence, and missed his wise conversation, but none so much as Pericles, who never forgot him, and who gave him money enough to keep him in comfort.

Another great friend of Pericles was a woman called As-pa´sia. She was so bright that the wisest men of Athens used to go to her house merely for the pleasure of talking to her. All the best-informed people in town used to assemble there; and Cimon and Pericles, Phidias, Anaxagoras, and Soc´ra-tes were among her chosen friends.

LX. BEGINNING OF THE PELOPONNESIAN WAR.

The end of Pericles' long and useful life was troubled by a new war between Athens and Sparta; for, as soon as the thirty-years' truce was ended, both cities flew to arms. The war which then began, and which in history is known as the Peloponnesian War, lasted almost as long as the truce; that is to say, for nearly thirty years.

Pericles knew very well that the Athenians, not being so well trained, were no match for the Spartans on land. He therefore advised all the people to come into the city, and take refuge behind the mighty walls, while the fleet carried on the war by sea.

This advice was followed. All the farmers left their fields, and crowded into Athens. When the Spartans came into Attica, they found the farms and villages deserted; but from the top of the Acropolis the people could see the enemy burn down their empty dwellings and destroy the harvests in their fields.

In the mean while the Athenian fleet had sailed out of the Piræus, and had gone down into the Peloponnesus, where the troops landed from time to time, striking terror into the hearts of the inhabitants, and causing much damage.

The Spartans also had a fleet; but it was so much smaller than that of the Athenians, that it could not offer any very great resistance. Still the time came when a battle was to take place between the vessels of the two cities.

It happened on a day when there was to be an eclipse of the sun. Now, you know that this is a very simple and natural thing. An eclipse of the sun is a darkening of its surface, which occurs whenever the moon passes between it and the earth.

As the moon is a very large and solid body, we cannot see either through or around it, and for a few minutes while it is directly between us and the sun itentirely hides the latter from our sight. Pericles, who had so often talked with Anaxagoras and the other learned men of his day, knew what an eclipse was, and had even been told that one would soon take place. He was therefore quite ready for it, warned his soldiers that it was coming, and illustrated his meaning by flinging his cloak over the head of his pilot.

"Can you see the sun now?" he asked.—"Why, no! master, of course not!" replied the man. "Your thick cloak is between me and the sun; how could I see through it?"—"Well, neither can you see through the moon, then," replied Pericles.

His men, thus warned, showed no fear of the eclipse; but the Spartans, who did not trouble themselves greatly with learning, were terrified. They imagined that the darkening of the sun at midday was the sign of some coming misfortune, and hardly dared to fight against the Athenians.

Thanks to this superstitious fear, Pericles laid waste the fields of the Peloponnesus, and came back to Athens in triumph; for, although much damage had been done to the enemy, the Athenians had lost only a few men. These were buried with great honors. Pericles himself pronounced their funeral oration; and we are told that he was so eloquent that all his hearers were melted to tears.

LXI. DEATH OF PERICLES.

Although the Athenian fleet had caused much damage, and had come home victorious, the Spartan army was still in Attica. The Spartans had been awed and frightened by the eclipse, but they did not give up their purpose, and continued the war.

The Athenians remained within the city walls, not daring to venture out lest they should meet with a defeat, and they soon began to suffer greatly. As there were not enough water and food for the crowded multitude, a terrible disease called the plague soon attacked the people. This sickness was contagious, and it spread rapidly. On all sides one could see the dead and dying. The sufferers were tormented by a burning thirst; and as there was soon no one left to care for the sick, they painfully dragged themselves to the sides of the fountains, where many of them died.

Not only were the sick uncared for, but it was also nearly impossible to dispose of the dead; and the bodies lay in the streets day after day, waiting for burial.

When the Athenians were in the greatest distress, Pericles heard that there was a Greek doctor, named Hip-poc´ra-tes, who had a cure for the plague; and he wrote to him, imploring his help.

Hippocrates received Pericles' letter at the same time that a message arrived from Artaxerxes, King of Persia. The king asked him to come and save the Persians, who were suffering from the same disease, and offered the doctor great wealth.

The noble doctor did not hesitate a moment, but sent away the Persian messenger, saying that it was his duty first to save his own countrymen. Then he immediately set out for the plague-stricken city of Athens, where he worked bravely night and day.

His care and skill restored many sufferers; and, although thousands died of the plague, the remaining Athenians knew that they owed him their lives. When the danger was over, they all voted that Hippocrates should have a golden crown, and said he should be called an Athenian citizen,—an honor which they seldom granted to any outsider.

The plague had not only carried away many of the poorer citizens, but had also stricken down the nobles and the rich. Pericles' family suffered from it too. All his children took it and died, with the exception of one.

The great man, in spite of his private cares and sorrows, was always in and out among the people, helping and encouraging them, and he finally caught the plague himself.

His friends soon saw, that, in spite of all their efforts, he would die. They crowded around his bed in tears, praising him in low tones, and saying how much he had done for the Athenians and for the improvement of their city.

"Why," said one of them warmly, "he found the city bricks, and leaves it marble!"

Pericles, whose eyes had been closed, and who seemed unconscious, now suddenly roused himself, and said, "Why do you mention those things? They were mostly owing to my large fortune. The thing of which I am proudest is that I never caused any fellow-citizen to put on mourning!"

Pericles then sank back, and soon died; but his friends always remembered that he had ruled Athens for more than thirty years without ever punishing any one unjustly, and that he had always proved helpful and merciful to all.

LXII. THE PHILOSOPHER SOCRATES.

When Pericles died, the Peloponnesian War had already been carried on for more than three years, but was not nearly at an end. As the Athenians felt the need of a leader, they soon chose Nic´ias to take the place left vacant by Pericles.

This Nicias was an honest man; but he was unfortunately rather dull, and very slow about deciding anything. Whenever he was called upon to see to matters of state, he hesitated so long, and was so uncertain, that the Greeks often had cause to regret the loss of Pericles.

There was another man of note in Athens at this time, the philosopher Socrates, a truly wise and good man. He was no politician, however; and, instead of troubling himself about the state, he spent all his spare moments in studying, or in teaching the young men of Athens.

Like his friend Anaxagoras, Socrates was a very deep thinker. He, too, always tried to find out the exact truth about everything. He was specially anxious to know how the earth had been created, who the Being was who gave us life, and whether the soul died with the body, or continued to live after the body had fallen into dust.

Socrates was a poor man, a stonecutter by trade; but he spent every moment he could spare from his work in thinking, studying, and questioning others. Little by little, in spite of the contrary opinion of his fellow-citizens, he began to understand that the stories of the Greek gods and goddesses could not be true.

He thought that there must surely be a God far greater than they,—a God who was good and powerful and just, who governed the world he had created, and who rewarded the virtuous and punished the wicked.

Socrates believed that everybody should be as good and gentle as possible, and freely forgive all injuries. This belief was very different from that of all ancient nations, who, on the contrary, thought that they should try to avenge every insult, and return evil for evil.

The philosopher Socrates not only taught this gentleness, but practiced it carefully at home and abroad. He had plenty of opportunity to make use of it; for he had such a cross wife, that her name, Xan-thip´pe, is still used to describe a scolding and bad-tempered woman.

Socrates.

Whenever Xanthippe was angry, she used to scold poor Socrates roundly. He always listened without flying into a passion, or even answering her; and when her temper was too unbearable, he quietly left the house, and went about his business elsewhere.

This gentleness and meekness only angered Xanthippe the more; and one day, when he was escaping as usual, she caught up a jug full of water and poured it over his head.

Socrates good-naturedly shook off the water, smiled, and merely remarked to his companions, "After the thunder comes the rain."

LXIII. SOCRATES' FAVORITE PUPIL.

As you have already heard, Socrates was a teacher. He did not, however, have a school like yours, with desks, and books, and maps, and blackboards. His pupils gathered about him at his workshop, or in the cool porticoes, or under the trees in the garden of the Academy.

Then, while hammering his stone, or while slowly pacing up and down, the philosopher talked to his scholars so gently and wisely, that even the richest and noblest youths of Athens were proud to call him their teacher. He also visited the house of the noted Aspasia, and was a friend of Pericles, Phidias, and Anaxagoras, besides being the teacher of three very celebrated men,—Pla´to, Xen´o-phon, and Al-ci-bi´a-des.

Alcibiades dared the Driver to come on.

Plato and Xenophon, even in their youth, were noted for their coolness and right-mindedness; but Alcibiades, a general favorite, was very different from them both. He was an orphan, and the ward of Pericles. His father had left him a large fortune; and, as Alcibiades was handsome, intelligent, and very high-spirited, he was made much of and greatly spoiled.

Even as a little child he was very headstrong, and, as he had no father and mother to check him, he was often led by his willfulness into great danger. We are told that once, when he saw a wagon coming down the street where he and his playmates were playing, he called to the man to stop. The man, who cared nothing for their game, drove on, and the other children quickly sprang aside so as not to be run over. Alcibiades, however, flung himself down across the road, in front of his playthings, and dared the driver to come on.

This was of course very foolish; and if the driver had given him a few sharp cuts with his whip, it might have done Alcibiades a great deal of good. But the man was so amused by the little fellow's pluck, that he actually turned around and drove through another street.

When Alcibiades grew a little older, he went to listen to the teachings of Socrates. In the presence of this wise man, Alcibiades forgot all his vanity and willfulness, talked sensibly, and showed himself well informed and kind-hearted.

He seemed so earnest and simple that Socrates soon grew very fond of him. They often walked together on the street; and it must have been pleasing to see this tall, handsome, and aristocratic youth, eagerly listening tothe wise words of the homely, toil-worn workman beside him.

Unfortunately, however, Alcibiades could not pass all his time with the good philosopher, and when he left him it was to spend the rest of the day with his own class. As he was rich, generous, and handsome, his companions always flattered him, approved of all he did, and admired everything he said.

This constant flattery was very bad for the young man; and, as he was anxious to please everybody, it often led him to do foolish things. He gave costly banquets, drove fast horses, boasted a great deal, and even started out for his first battle in a magnificent suit of armor all inlaid with gold.

His shield was also inlaid with gold and ivory, and on it was a picture of Cu´pid throwing the thunderbolts of Jove (Zeus). All his flatterers, instead of telling him frankly that such armor was ridiculous, admired him greatly, and vowed that he looked like the god of the sun.

In the midst of the battle, Alcibiades, who was very brave, rushed into the thick of the foe. His armor was not as strong as a plainer suit would have been; and he soon found himself hemmed round, and almost ready to fall. His fine friends had of course deserted the lad; but, fortunately for him, Socrates was there. The philosopher rushed into the midst of the fray, caught up the young man in his strong arms, and bore him off the battlefield to a place of safety, where he tenderly bound up his wounds.

As Alcibiades was a good-hearted youth, he felt deeply grateful to Socrates for saving his life, and ever after proudly claimed him as a friend. In spite of the philosopher's advice, however, the young man continued to frequent the same society; and, as he was genial and open-handed with all, he daily grew more popular.

LXIV. YOUTH OF ALCIBIADES.

As the Greeks all loved the Olympic games, Alcibiades was always seen there. He took part in the chariot races especially; and his horses won three prizes in succession, to the delight of his admirers.

Alcibiades was shrewd enough, in spite of all his vanity, to understand that the people of Athens loved him principally because he was handsome and rich. He also knew that they delighted in gossip, and he sometimes did a thing merely to hear them talk about it.

He had a very handsome dog, for instance; and for a little while its beauty was praised by every one. But the Athenians soon grew used to the animal, and ceased to talk about it. Then Alcibiades had the dog's tail cut off, and of course every one began to exclaim about that.

Some of the Athenians became so inquisitive that they asked why he had done so, and he laughingly answered that it was merely in order to supply them with material for conversation and wonder.

Alcibiades was so merry and light-hearted that he treated even serious matters in a joking way. We are told, that, when he was first admitted to the city council, he acted like a schoolboy, and mischievously let loose a captive quail, which ran in and out among the feet of the councilors, and fluttered about so wildly as to upset the gravity of the whole assembly.

On another occasion the councilors were all waiting for Alcibiades to begin their proceedings. He entered the hall with a crown of flowers on his head; begged them to excuse him, because he could really not attend to business, as he had a banquet at his house; and asked them to adjourn and go home with him.

Strange to relate, his manner was so fascinating that the grave councilors did as he wished, and dropped their important business to feast with him. It was on account of this influence that an Athenian citizen once bitterly exclaimed, "Go on, my brave boy! Your prosperity will bring ruin on this crowd."

Alcibiades was such a favorite among rich and poor, that the Athenians would gladly have made him king. Fortunately, however, the young man still had sense enough to refuse this honor; but, although he would not accept the title, he exercised much of the power of a king, and soon he and Nicias were the principal politicians of the day.

Alcibiades was as ambitious as Nicias was careful; and while the latter was always trying to keep the Athenians as quiet and contented as possible, Alcibiades was always ready to think of some plan by which the power of the city could be extended.

This ambition of Alcibiades was destined to have a very bad effect upon his own fortunes and upon those of his native land, as you will see by the end of his career.

LXV. GREEK COLONIES IN ITALY.

The Greeks, as you know, had founded colonies all along the coast of Asia Minor and on many of the islands. They had also sailed as far as Italy and Sicily, where they built many towns.

Little by little these colonies grew richer and stronger. As the Greek settlers increased in number, they claimed more and more land. In Sicily and southern Italy the soil was so fertile that the people soon grew very rich; and, as they had vessels in plenty, they traded everywhere, and became noted for their commercial enterprise.

The first of the Greek colonies in southern Italy was the city of Syb´a-ris. It was so prosperous that the people had more money than they knew what to do with; and they spent large sums in making their houses beautiful and in securing every comfort.

The Syb´a-rites soon became so luxurious in their habits, that they were noted all over the country for their love of ease. We are told that one Sybarite, for instance, once ordered his slaves to prepare a couch for him of fresh rose leaves.

When it was ready, he stretched himself out upon it and slept. In a short time he awoke with cries of great distress, saying that he could not sleep because a rose leaf was crumpled under him, and chafed his tender skin.

Ever since then, when people make a great fuss about a trifle, they are apt to hear the remark, "'Tis the crumpled rose leaf!" and when they spend too much thought upon their bodily comfort, and indulge in too much luxury, they are called Sybarites.

The people of this town continued to flourish for some time, but they finally quarreled with the neighboring colony of Croton. A war followed, in which the ease-loving Sybarites were defeated and their city was destroyed.

Croton and Ta-ren´tum on the mainland, and Messina and Syr´a-cuse on the Island of Sicily, were now the principal colonies. They were all very rich and prosperous, so Alcibiades told the Athenians that it would be a good plan to send out a fleet to conquer and annex them.

Nicias and his party opposed this plan; but when it was put to the vote, it was found that the eloquence of Alcibiades had prevailed. A large fleet was prepared, and Nicias, Lam´a-chus, and Alcibiades were chosen generals of the expedition. The fleet was on the point of sailing out of the Piræus, when the Athenians found out that all the statues of their god Her´mes, which were used as boundary marks and milestones, had been shamefully broken.

The excited people assembled on the market place to discuss this event; and all cried loudly against it, for the statues were considered sacred, as they represented a god. Alcibiades' enemies—and he had a number, although he was so popular—now stepped forward, and declared that he had done it after the banquet which he had given to celebrate his departure.

The young man denied having broken the statues, and asked that his trial might take place at once, so that he might prove his innocence before he started out; but, in spite of this urgent request, it was postponed, and he was forced to depart with this cloud hanging over him.

LXVI. ALCIBIADES IN DISGRACE.

Alcibiades had no sooner sailed, however, than his enemies, grown bolder, began to talk louder, and soon convinced the people of his guilt. In their wrath, the Athenians now sent a messenger to Sicily to overtake him, and bid him return to Athens to be tried.

His friends, seeing the excitement of the people, and fearing that they would condemn him in anger, sent word to him not to return, but to wait until the popular fury had had time to blow over.

In obedience to this advice, Alcibiades left the fleet, and, instead of going to Athens, went straight to Sparta, where he took up his abode. Here the changeable youth adopted the Spartan dress, lived with the utmost simplicity and frugality, and even used the laconic mode of speech.

As he was tall and strong, and a very good athlete, he soon won the admiration of the Spartans, and made many friends. During his stay here, he heard that he had been tried at Athens, although absent, found guilty of sacrilege, and even sentenced to death.

This ingratitude on the part of his people so angered Alcibiades, that he told the Spartans all the Athenian plans, and showed how to upset them. By his advice, the Spartans sent aid to the Greeks in Sicily, helped them to resist the Athenian attack, and even captured both generals and seven thousand soldiers, who were put to death.

Alcibiades.

The Spartans, still under Alcibiades' instructions, now took and fortified the small town of Dec-e-le´a, only twelve miles from Athens. Here they kept an armed force, ready to spring out at any minute and molest the Athenians, who thus found themselves in a continual state of warfare and insecurity.

The small cities and islands which the Athenians had won by force now seized this favorable opportunity to revolt; and the Persians, at Alcibiades' invitation, joined them, and again began to wage war with the proud city.

The Athenians were almost in despair. They had enemies on all sides, and were also worried by the quarrels of aristocrats and democrats within the city. These two political parties were now so opposed to each other, that nothing could make them friends.

The army, longing for action, and without a leader, finally took matters into their own hands. They recalled Alcibiades, and asked him to help them. The young man, who was generous and kind-hearted, immediately responded to this appeal; and, now that it was too late, he repented of what he had done, and began to do all in his power to defeat the enemy he had aroused.

By his eloquence and skill, Alcibiades finally succeeded in winning the Persians over to side with the Athenians, and to fight against the Spartans; but all his efforts to make up for the past were vain. His treachery had ruined Athens; and when he led the troops against the Spartans, the

Athenians were completely defeated.

LXVII. DEATH OF ALCIBIADES.

Afraid to return to his native city, where he knew the people would blame him for their sufferings, Alcibiades fled. After roaming about for some time, he took refuge in a castle which he had built on the Cher-so-ne´sus.

From the height upon which the castle stood, Alcibiades could overlook the sea on both sides; and he watched the Spartan and Athenian fleets, which, unknown to each other, had come to anchor very near him. He soon discovered that the Spartans had become aware of the presence of the Athenians, and were preparing to surprise them.

He therefore left his castle, and, at the risk of his life, went down to warn the Athenians of the coming danger. They, however, treated his warning with scorn, and bade him return to his castle, and remember that he no longer had any right to interfere in their affairs.

From the top of his promontory, Alcibiades saw the complete destruction of the Athenian fleet. Only a few men managed to escape to his castle for shelter; while a single ship sailed in haste to Athens, to report the defeat, and warn the people of the coming danger.

A few days later the victorious Spartan army marched unchallenged into Athens, for there were now no fighting men left to oppose them. The Spartans said that Athens must now obey them in all things; and, to humiliate the people, they tore down the Long Walls to the sound of joyful music on the anniversary of the glorious victory of Salamis.

Thus ended the Peloponnesian War, which, as you have seen, began shortly before the death of Pericles. From this time on, the fame of Athens was due mostly to her literature and art.

By order of the Spartans, Solon's laws were set aside, and thirty men were chosen to govern the city. These rulers proved so stern and cruel, that they were soon known as the Thirty Tyrants, and were hated by every one.

The Athenians suffered so sorely under the government which the Spartans had thus forced upon them, that they soon began to long for the return of Alcibiades, who, whatever his faults, was always generous.

When the Thirty Tyrants and the Spartans learned of this feeling, they were afraid that the Athenians would summon Alcibiades, so they bribed the Persian governor to put him to death.

A party of murderers went to his house at night, and set it afire. Alcibiades, waking up suddenly, tried to escape with his household; but no sooner had he reached the door than he found himself surrounded by enemies.

Alcibiades quickly wrapped his cloak around his left arm to serve as a shield, and, seizing his sword in his right hand, rushed manfully out upon his foes. The Persians, frightened at his approach, fled in haste; but they came to a stop at a safe distance, and flung so many stones and spears at him that he soon fell dead from the blows.

His body was left where it had fallen, and was found by his wife, who loved him dearly in spite of all his faults. She tenderly wrapped it up in her own mantle, and had it buried not far from where it lay.

Thus ended the life of the brilliant Alcibiades, who died at the age of forty, far away from his native land, and from the people whose idol he had once been, but whom he had ruined by his vanity.

LXVIII. THE OVERTHROW OF THE THIRTY TYRANTS.

Although the Thirty Tyrants ruled in Athens but a short time, they condemned fifteen hundred men to death, and drove many good citizens into exile. During their brief period of authority they even found fault with Socrates, and would have liked to kill him, though he was the greatest philosopher the world has ever known.

As the rule of the Thirty Tyrants had been forced upon them by the victorious Spartans, the Athenians soon resolved to get rid of them. Among the good citizens whom these cruel rulers had driven away into exile, was Thras-y-bu´lus, who was a real patriot.

He had seen the sufferings of the Athenians, and his sympathy had been roused. So he began plotting against the Thirty Tyrants, assembled a few brave men, entered the city, drove out the Spartans, and overturned their government when they least expected it.

Some years later the Athenians rebuilt the Long Walls, which Ly-san´der, the Spartan general, had torn down to the sound of festive music. They were so glad to be rid of the cruel tyrants, that they erected statues in honor of Thrasybulus, their deliverer, and sang songs in his praise at all their public festivals.

The Spartans, in the mean while, had been changing rapidly for the worse, for the defeat of the Athenians had filled their hearts with pride, and had made them fancy they were the bravest and greatest people on earth. Such conceit is always harmful.

Lysander, in capturing Athens and the smaller towns of Attica, had won much booty, which was all sent to Sparta. The ephors refused at first to accept or distribute this gold, saying that the love of wealth was the root of all evil; but they finally decided to use it for the improvement of their city.

Lysander himself was as noble a man as he was a good general, and kept none of the booty for his own use. On the contrary, he came back to Sparta so poor, that, when he died, the city had to pay his funeral expenses.

The Spartans felt so grateful for the services which he had rendered them, that they not only gave him a fine burial, but also gave marriage portions to his daughters, and helped them to get good husbands.

LXIX. ACCUSATION OF SOCRATES.

Socrates, as you know, was one of the best and gentlest of men, yet he had many enemies. These were principally the people who were jealous of him and of his renown for great wisdom; for his reputation was so well established, that the oracle at Delphi, when consulted, replied that the most learned man in Greece was Socrates.

Although Socrates was so wise and good and gentle, he was not at all conceited, and showed his wisdom by never pretending to know what he did not know, and by his readiness to learn anything new, provided one could prove it to be true.

Among the noted Athenians of this time was Aristophanes, a writer of comedies or funny plays. He was so witty that his comedies are still admired almost as much as when they were played in the Theater of Dionysus for the amusement of the people.

Like most funny men, Aristophanes liked to turn everything into ridicule. He had often seen Socrates and Alcibiades walking through the streets of Athens, and was greatly amused at the contrast they presented.

Now, Aristophanes, with all his cleverness, was not always just; and while his ridicule sometimes did good, at other times it did a great deal of harm. He soon learned to dislike Alcibiades; but he saw how dearly the people loved the young man, and fancied that his faults must be owing to the bad advice of his teacher. Such was not the case, for Socrates had tried to bring out all the good in his pupil. Alcibiades' pride, insolence, and treachery were rather the result of the constant flattery to which he had been exposed on the part of those who claimed to be his friends.

Aristophanes disliked Alcibiades so much that he soon wrote a comedy called "The Clouds," in which he made fun of him. Of course, he did not call the people in the play by their real names; but the hero was a good-for-nothing young man, who, advised by his teacher, bought fast horses, ran his father into debt, cheated everybody, and treated even the gods with disrespect.

As the actors who took part in this comedy dressed and acted as nearly as possible like Alcibiades and Socrates, you can imagine that the play, which was very comical and clever, made the Athenians roar with laughter.

Everybody talked about it, repeated the best jokes, and went again and again to see and laugh over it. We are told that Socrates went there himself one day; and, when asked why he had come, he quietly said, "I came to find out whether, among all the faults of which I am accused, there may not be some that I can correct."

You see, the philosopher knew that it was never too late to mend, and fully intended to be as perfect as possible. He knew, of course, that he could not straighten his crooked nose or make his face good-looking, but he hoped to find some way of improving his character.

"The Clouds" amused the Athenians for about twenty years; and when Alcibiades turned traitor, and caused the ruin of his country, the people still went to see it. In their anger against Alcibiades, they began to think that perhaps Aristophanes was right, and that the youth they had once loved so dearly would never have turned out so badly had he not been influenced for evil.

As the teacher in the play was blamed for all the wrongdoing of his pupil, so Socrates was now accused by the Athenians of ruining Alcibiades. Little by little the philosopher's enemies became so bold that they finally made up their minds to get rid of him. As he was quite innocent, and as there was no other excuse for dragging him before the Tribunal, they finally charged him with giving bad advice to young men, and speaking ill of the gods.

LXX. DEATH OF SOCRATES.

The false accusation made against Socrates by his enemies soon had the desired effect, for the Tribunal gave orders for his arrest and trial. The philosopher, sure of his innocence, came before his judges, and calmly answered their questions.

He told them he had never turned the gods into ridicule, as he knew it was wrong to make fun of anything which others deemed sacred. Then, as they still further pressed him to explain his views, he confessed that he believed there was a God greater and better than any they worshiped.

As to teaching the young men anything which could do them harm, he said it was quite impossible; for he had ever told them that they should be as good, virtuous, and helpful as they could, which was surely not wrong.

Socrates gave noble answers to all their questions; but the judges, blinded with prejudice, believed the lying charges of his enemies, which Socrates scorned to contradict. The philosopher's friends begged him to use his eloquence to defend himself and confound his accusers; but he calmly refused, saying, "My whole life and teaching is the only contradiction, and the best defense I can offer."

Socrates, as you have seen, was really one of the best men that ever lived, and, without having ever heard of the true God, he still believed in him. Nearly four centuries before the coming of

Christ, when people believed in revenge, he preached the doctrine of "Love one another" and "Do good to them that hate you."

But, in spite of all his goodness and constant uprightness, Socrates the philosopher was condemned to the shameful death of a base criminal.

Now, in Greece, criminals were forced to drink a cup of deadly poison at sunset on the day of their condemnation, and there was generally but a few hours' delay between the sentence and its execution. But the law said that during one month in the year no such punishment should be inflicted. This was while an Athenian vessel was away on a voyage to the Island of De'los to bear the annual offerings to Apollo's shrine.

As Socrates was tried and condemned at this season, the people were forced to await the return of the vessel before they could kill him: so they put him in prison. Here he was chained fast, yet his friends were allowed to visit him and to talk with him.

Day after day the small band of his pupils gathered around him in prison; and, as some of them were very rich, they bribed the jailer, and arranged everything for their beloved master's escape.

When the time came, and Socrates was told that he could leave the prison unseen, and be taken to a place of safety, he refused to go, saying that it would be against the law, which he had never yet disobeyed.

In vain his friends and disciples begged him to save his life: he would not consent. Then Cri'to, one of his pupils, began to weep, in his distress, and exclaimed indignantly, "Master, will you then remain here, and die innocent?"

"Of course," replied Socrates, gravely. "Would you rather I should die guilty?"

Then, gathering his disciples around him, he began to talk to them in the most beautiful and solemn way about life and death, and especially about the immortality of the soul.

This last conversation of Socrates was so attentively listened to by his disciple Plato, the wisest among them all, that he afterward wrote it down from memory almost word for word, and thus kept it so that we can still read it.

Socrates' Farewell.

As the sun was slowly setting on that last day, the sacred vessel came back from Delos. The time of waiting was ended, and now the prisoner must die. The jailer interrupted this beautiful last talk, and entered the cell, bringing the cup of poison.

Socrates took the cup from his hand and drained it, unmoved, telling his disciples that he felt sure that death was only birth into another and better world. Then he bade them all farewell.

As he was a good and scrupulous man, very careful about paying his debts and keeping his promises, he now told Crito to remember that he had promised to sacrifice a cock to Æs-cu-la´pi-us, the god of medicine, and bade him do it in his stead.

He then lay down upon his hard prison bed, and, while he felt the chill of death slowly creeping upward toward his heart, he continued to teach and exhort his pupils to love virtue and do right.

All his last sayings were carefully treasured by Plato, who wrote them down, and who concludes the story of his death in these beautiful words: "Thus died the man who, of all with whom we are acquainted, was in death the noblest, and in life the wisest and best."

Some time after the death of Socrates, the Athenians found out their mistake. Filled with remorse, they recalled the sentence which had condemned him, but they could not bring him back to life. In token of their sorrow, however, they set up a statue of him in the heart of their city.

This statue, although made of bronze, has long ceased to exist; but the remembrance of Socrates' virtues is still held dear, and all who know his name both love and honor him.

LXXI. THE DEFEAT OF CYRUS.

It was at the close of the Peloponnesian War that Darius II., King of Persia, died, leaving two sons, Artaxerxes and Cy´rus. These two heirs could not agree which should reign. Artaxerxes claimed the throne because he was the elder, and Cyrus because he was the first son born after their father had become king; for in Persia it was the custom for a ruler to choose as his successor a son born after he had taken possession of the throne.

The quarrel between the two brothers daily became more bitter; and when Artaxerxes made himself king by force, Cyrus swore that he would compel him to give up his place again.

To oust his brother from the throne, Cyrus collected an army in Asia Minor; and, as he could not secure enough Persian soldiers, he hired a body of eleven thousand Greeks, commanded by a Spartan named Cle-ar´chus.

This Greek army was only a small part of Cyrus' force; but he expected great things from it, as the Persians had already found out to their cost that the Greeks were very good fighters.

After a long march, the armies of both brothers met at Cu-nax´a; and there was a terrible battle, in the midst of which Cyrus was killed. Of course, his death ended the quarrel, and the Persians all surrendered.

But the Greeks continued fighting bravely, until Artaxerxes sent them word that his brother was dead, and that he would have them guided safely back to their own country if they would lay down their arms.

The Greeks, believing him, immediately stopped fighting; and their officers accepted an invitation to enter the Persian camp, and be present at the council of all the generals.

Their trust was sadly misplaced, however; for no sooner had the Greek officers entered the tent than they were surrounded and slain. The Persian king then sent a message to the Greek troops, saying that their leaders were all dead, and summoning them to give up their arms and to swear to obey him in all things.

This message filled the hearts of the Greeks with rage and despair. What were they to do? Their chiefs were dead, they were in a strange country surrounded by enemies, and their own home lay eight months' journey away.

They had no leaders, no money or provisions, and no guides to show them the way back across the burning sands, deep rivers, and over the mountains. They had nothing, in short, but the armor on their backs and the weapons in their hands.

As they did not even know the language of the country, they could not ask their way; and as they were surrounded by enemies, they must be constantly on their guard lest they should be surprised and taken prisoners or killed. They were indeed in a sorry plight; and no wonder that they all fancied they would never see their homes again. When night came on, they flung themselves down upon the ground without having eaten any supper. Their hearts were so heavy, however, that they could not sleep, but tossed and moaned in their despair.

In this army there was a pupil of Socrates, called Xenophon. He was a good and brave man. Instead of bewailing his bad luck, as the others did, he tried to think of some plan by which the army might yet be saved, and brought back to Greece.

His night of deep thought was not in vain; and as soon as morning dawned he called his companions together, and begged them to listen to him, as he had found a way of saving them from slavery or death.

Then he explained to them, that, if they were only united and willing, they could form a compact body, and, under a leader of their own choosing, could beat a safe retreat toward the sea.

LXXII. THE RETREAT OF THE TEN THOUSAND.

Xenophon's advice pleased the Greeks. It was far better, they thought, to make the glorious attempt to return home, than basely to surrender their arms, and become the subjects of a foreign king.

They therefore said they would elect a leader, and all chose Xenophon to fill this difficult office. He, however, consented to accept it only upon condition that each soldier would pledge his word of honor to obey him; for he knew that the least disobedience would hinder success, and that in union alone lay strength. The soldiers understood this too, and not only swore to obey him, but even promised not to quarrel among themselves.

So the little army began its homeward march, tramping bravely over sandy wastes and along rocky pathways. When they came to a river too deep to be crossed by fording, they followed it up toward its source until they could find a suitable place to get over it; and, as they had neither money nor provisions, they were obliged to seize all their food on the way.

The Greeks not only had to overcome countless natural obstacles, but were also compelled to keep up a continual warfare with the Persians who pursued them. Every morning Xenophon had to draw up his little army in the form of a square, to keep the enemy at bay.

They would fight thus until nearly nightfall, when the Persians always retreated, to camp at a distance from the men they feared. Instead of allowing his weary soldiers to sit down and rest, Xenophon would then give orders to march onward. So they tramped in the twilight until it was too dark or they were too tired to proceed any farther.

After a hasty supper, the Greeks flung themselves down to rest on the hard ground, under the light of the stars; but even these slumbers were cut short by Xenophon's call at early dawn. Long before the lazy Persians were awake, these men were again marching onward; and when the mounted enemy overtook them once more, and compelled them to halt and fight, they were several miles nearer home.

As the Greeks passed through the wild mountain gorges, they were further hindered by the neighboringpeople, who tried to stop them by rolling trunks of trees and rocks down upon them. Although some were wounded and others killed, the little army pressed forward, and, after a march of about a thousand miles, they came at last within sight of the sea.

You may imagine what a joyful shout arose, and how lovingly they gazed upon the blue waters which washed the shores of their native land also.

But although Xenophon and his men had come to the sea, their troubles were not yet ended; for, as they had no money to pay their passage, none of the captains would take them on board.

Instead of embarking, therefore, and resting their weary limbs while the wind wafted them home, they were forced to tramp along the seashore. They were no longer in great danger, but were tired and discontented, and now for the first time they began to forget their promise to obey Xenophon.

To obtain money enough to pay their passage to Greece, they took several small towns along their way, and robbed them. Then, hearing that there was a new expedition on foot to free the Ionian cities from the Persian yoke, they suddenly decided not to return home, but to go and help them.

Xenophon therefore led them to Per´ga-mus, where he gave them over to their new leader. There were still ten thousand left out of the eleven thousand men that Cyrus had hired, and Xenophon had cause to feel proud of having brought them across the enemy's territory with so little loss.

After bidding them farewell, Xenophon returned home, and wrote down an account of this famous Retreat of the Ten Thousand in a book called the A-nab´a-sis. This account is so interesting that people begin to read it as soon as they know a little Greek, and thus learn all about the fighting and marching of those brave men.

LXXIII. AGESILAUS IN ASIA.

You may remember that the Greeks, at the end of the Peloponnesian War, had found out that Sparta was the strongest city in the whole country; for, although the Athenians managed to drive the Spartans out of their city, they were still forced to recognize them as the leaders of all Greece.

The Spartans were proud of having reached such a position, and were eager to maintain it at any cost. They therefore kept all the Greek towns under their orders, and were delighted to think that their king, A-ges-i-la'us, was one of the best generals of his day.

He was not, however, tall and strong, like most of his fellow-citizens, but puny and very lame. His small size and bad health had not lessened his courage, however, and he was always ready to plan a new campaign or to lead his men off to war.

When it became known that Artaxerxes was about to march against the Greek cities in Ionia, to punish them for upholding his brother Cyrus, and for sending him the ten thousand soldiers who had beat such a masterly retreat, Agesilaus made up his mind to go and help them.

There was no prospect of fighting at home just then, so the Spartan warriors were only too glad to follow their king to Asia. Agesilaus had no sooner landed in Asia Minor, than the Greek cities there gave him command over their army, bidding him defend them from the wrath of Artaxerxes.

Now, although the Persian host, as usual, far outnumbered the Greek army, Agesilaus won several victories over his enemies, who were amazed that such a small and insignificant-looking man should be at the same time a king and a great general.

They were accustomed to so much pomp and ceremony, and always saw their own king so richly dressed, that it seemed very queer to them to see Agesilaus going about in the same garments as his men, and himself leading them in battle.

LXXIV. A STRANGE INTERVIEW.

We are told that Agesilaus was once asked to meet the Persian general Phar-na-ba'zus, to have a talk or conference with him,—a thing which often took place between generals of different armies.

The meeting was set for a certain day and hour, under a large tree, and it was agreed that both generals should come under the escort of their personal attendants only.

Agesilaus, plainly clad as usual, came first to the meeting place, and, sitting down upon the grass under the tree, he began to eat his usual noonday meal of bread and onions.

Agesilaus and Pharnabazus.

A few moments later the Persian general arrived in rich attire, attended by fan and parasol bearer, and by servants bringing carpets for him to sit upon, cooling drinks to refresh him, and delicate dishes to tempt his appetite.

At first Pharnabazus fancied that a tramp was camping under the tree; but when he discovered that this plain little man was really Agesilaus, King of Sparta, and the winner of so many battles, he was ashamed of his pomp, sent away his attendants, and sat down on the ground beside the king.

They now began an important talk, and Pharnabazus was filled with admiration when he heard the short but noble answers which Agesilaus had for all his questions. He was so impressed by the Spartan king, that he shook hands with him when the interview was ended.

Agesilaus was equally pleased with Pharnabazus, and told him that he should be proud to call him friend. He invited him to leave his master, and come and live in Greece, where all noble men were free.

Pharnabazus did not accept this invitation, but renewed the war, whereupon Agesilaus again won several important victories. When the Persian king heard that all his soldiers could not get the better of the Spartan king, he resolved to try the effect of bribery.

He therefore sent a messenger to Athens to promise this city and her allies a very large sum of money provided that they would rise up in revolt against Sparta, and thus force Agesilaus to come home.

LXXV. THE PEACE OF ANTALCIDAS.

The Athenians hated the Spartans, and were only waiting for an excuse to make war against them: so they were only too glad to accept the bribe which Artaxerxes offered, and were paid with ten thousand Persian coins on which was stamped the figure of an archer.

As soon as the Spartan ephors heard that the Athenians had revolted, they sent a message to Agesilaus to tell him to come home. The Spartan king was about to deal a crushing blow to the Persians, but he was forced to obey the summons. As he embarked he dryly said, "I could easily have beaten the whole Persian army, and still ten thousand Persian archers have forced me to give up all my plans."

The Thebans joined the Athenians in this revolt, so Agesilaus was very indignant against them too. He energetically prepared for war, and met the combined Athenian and Theban forces at Coronea, where he defeated them completely.

The Athenians, in the mean while, had made their alliance with the Persians, and used the money which they had received to strengthen their ramparts, as you have seen, and to finish the Long Walls, which had been ruined by the Spartans ten years before.

All the Greek states were soon in arms, siding with the Athenians or with the Spartans; and the contest continued until everybody was weary of fighting. There was, besides, much jealousy among the people themselves, and even the laurels of Agesilaus were envied.

The person who was most opposed to him was the Spartan An-tal´ci-das, who, fearing that further warfare would only result in increasing Agesilaus' popularity and glory, now began to advise peace. As the Greeks were tired of the long struggle, they sent Antalcidas to Asia to try to make a treaty with the Persians.

Without thinking of anything but his hatred of Agesilaus, Antalcidas consented to all that the Persians asked, and finally signed a shameful treaty, by which all the Greek cities of Asia Minor and the Island of Cy´prus were handed over to the Persian king. The other Greek cities were declared independent, and thus Sparta was shorn of much of her power. This treaty was a disgrace, and it has always been known in history by the name of the man who signed it out of petty spite.

LXXVI. THE THEBAN FRIENDS.

Although all the Greek cities were to be free by the treaty of Antalcidas, the Spartans kept the Messenians under their sway and, as they were still the most powerful people in Greece, they saw that the other cities did not infringe upon their rights in any way.

Under pretext of keeping all their neighbors in order, the Spartans were always under arms, and on one occasion even forced their way into the city of Thebes. The Thebans, who did not expect them, were not ready to make war, and were in holiday dress.

They were all in the temple, celebrating the festival of Demeter, the harvest goddess; and when the Spartans came thus upon them, they were forced to yield without striking a single blow, as they had no weapons at hand.

The Spartans were so afraid lest the best and richest citizens should try to make the people revolt, that they exiled them all from Thebes, allowing none but the poor and insignificant to remain.

To keep possession of the city which they had won by this trick, the Spartans put three thousand of their best warriors in the citadel, with orders to defend and hold it at any price.

Among the exiled Thebans there was a noble and wealthy man called Pe-lop´i-das. He had been sorely wounded in a battle some time before, and would have died had he not been saved by a fellow-citizen named E-pam-i-non´das, who risked his own life in the rescue.

This man, too, was of noble birth, and was said to be a descendant of the men who had sprung from the dragon teeth sown by Cadmus, the founder of Thebes. Epaminondas, however, was very poor; and wealth had no charms for him, for he was a disciple of Py-tha´o-ras, a philosopher who was almost as celebrated as Socrates.

Now, although Epaminondas was poor, quiet, and studious, and Pelopidas was particularly fond of noise and bustle, they became great friends and almost inseparable companions. Pelopidas, seeing how good and generous a man his friend was, did all he could to be like him, and even gave up all his luxurious ways to live plainly too.

He therefore had plenty of money to spare, and this he spent very freely for the good of the poor. When his former friends asked why he no longer cared for his riches, he pointed to a poor cripple near by, and said that money was of importance only to unhappy men like that one, who could do nothing for themselves.

LXXVII. THEBES FREE ONCE MORE.

The Spartans, coming into Thebes, as we have seen, exiled the rich and important Pelopidas, but allowed his friend Epaminondas to remain. They little suspected that this quiet and seemingly stupid man would in time become their greatest enemy, and that the mere sound of his name would fill their hearts with dread.

Pelopidas, thus forced to leave home, withdrew to Athens, where he was very kindly received. He was not happy, however, and was always longing to return home, and see his friend Epaminondas, whose society he missed very much.

He therefore called a few of the Theban exiles together, and proposed that they should return to Thebes in disguise, and, taking advantage of the Spartans' carelessness, kill their leaders, and restore the city to freedom.

This proposal was received with joy, although the Spartans numbered three thousand, and the Theban exiles only twelve. The chances were of course against them; but the men were so anxious to free their city, that they resolved to make the attempt.

They therefore set out from Athens with weapons and hunting dogs, as if bent upon a day's sport in the country.Thus armed, they secretly entered the house of Cha´ron, one of their friends in Thebes. Here they exchanged their hunting garments for women's robes; for, hearing that the Spartan general and his officers were feasting, they had resolved to pretend that they were dancing girls, in order to gain an entrance into the banquet hall, and kill the men while they were drinking.

They had just finished dressing, when a knock was heard at the door, and a Spartan soldier came in and gravely informed Charon that the commander wished to see him.

For a moment Pelopidas and his companions fancied that their plans were discovered, and that

Charon had betrayed them. He read this suspicion in their frightened faces, and, before leaving the house with the soldier, he placed his only son, a mere infant, in the arms of Pelopidas, saying, "There, keep him; and if you find that I have betrayed you, avenge yourselves by killing my only child, my dearest treasure."

After speaking thus, Charon went out, and soon came back to report that all was well.

The Theban exiles now went to the banquet hall, where they were readily allowed to enter to amuse the company. The Spartan officers, who were no longer frugal and temperate as of old, were so heavy and stupid with wine, that the supposed dancing girls easily killed them.

"Avenge yourselves by killing my only child."

One version of the story is, that Pelopidas and his companions rushed out into the street with lighted torches, and slew every Spartan they met. The Spartan soldiers, deprived of most of their officers (who had been killed in the banquet hall), and greatly frightened, fled in the darkness from what they fancied was a large army, and returned in haste to Sparta.

Imagine their shame, however, when it became known there that they had been routed by only twelve determined men! The Spartan citizens were so angry that they put the two remaining officers to death, and, collecting another army, placed it under the leadership of Cle-om'bro-tus, their second king, because Agesilaus was too ill at the time to fight.

LXXVIII. THE BATTLE OF LEUCTRA.

The Thebans, delighted at having thus happily got rid of their enemies, had made Pelopidas and Epaminondas Bœ'o-tarchs, or chiefs of Bœotia, the country of which Thebes was the capital. These two men, knowing well that the Spartans would soon send an army to win back the city, now made great preparations to oppose them.

Epaminondas was made general of the army; and Pelopidas drilled a choice company, called the Sacred Battalion. This was formed of three hundred brave young Thebans, who took a solemn oath never to turn their backs upon the enemy or to surrender, and to die for their native country if necessary.

The Thebans then marched forth to meet their foes; and the two armies met at Leuc'tra, a small town in Bœotia. As usual, the Thebans had consulted the oracles to find out what they should do, and had been told that all the omens were unfavorable. Epaminondas, however, nobly replied that he knew of none which forbade fighting for the defense of one's country, and he boldly ordered the attack.

The Spartans were greatly amused when they heard that Epaminondas, a student, was the commander of the army, and they expected to win a very easy victory. They were greatly surprised, therefore, when their onslaught was met firmly, and when, in spite of all their valor, they found themselves defeated, and heard that their leader, Cleombrotus, was dead.

The Thebans, of course, gloried in their triumph; but Epaminondas remained as modest and unassuming as ever, merely remarking that he was glad for his country's and parents' sake that he had been successful. To commemorate their good fortune, the Thebans erected a trophy on the battlefield of Leuctra, where their troops had covered themselves with glory.

The inhabitants of Sparta, who had counted confidently upon victory, were dismayed when they saw only a few of their soldiers return from the battle, and heard that the Thebans were pursuing them closely. Before they could collect new troops, the enemy marched boldly down into Laconia; and the women of Sparta now beheld the smoke of the enemy's camp for the first time in many years. As there were neither walls nor fortifications of any kind, you can easily imagine that the inhabitants were in despair, and thought that their last hour had come.

If Epaminondas had been of a revengeful temper, he could easily have destroyed the city; but he was gentle and humane, and, remaining at a short distance from the place, he said that he would go away without doing the Spartans any harm, provided they would promise not to attack Thebes again, and to set the Messenians free.

These conditions were eagerly agreed to by the Spartans, who found themselves forced to take a secondary place once more. Athens had ruled Greece, and had been forced to yield to Sparta; but now Sparta was compelled in her turn to recognize the supremacy of Thebes.

LXXIX. DEATH OF PELOPIDAS.

Thebes was the main power in Greece after the brilliant victory at Leuctra, and for a short time the city managed to maintain its supremacy. By virtue of its position, it decided the destiny of less powerful cities; and when Al-ex-an´der, tyrant of Thessaly, became very cruel, the Thebans sent Pelopidas to remonstrate with him.

Instead of treating the ambassador of the Thebans with courtesy, however, the Thessalian tyrant loaded him with heavy chains, put him in prison, and vowed he would keep him there as long as he lived.

When the news of this outrage reached the Thebans, they set out at once, under the guidance of two new Bœotarchs, to deliver their beloved fellow-citizen. Epaminondas, too, marched in the ranks; for, now that his term of office was ended, he had contentedly returned to his former obscure position.

The new Bœotarchs were unfortunately very poor generals. They met the Thessalian army, but were defeated and driven back. Indeed, the Thebans were soon in such danger, that the soldiers revolted against their generals, and begged Epaminondas again to take the lead.

As they were in great distress, Epaminondas could not refuse to help them: so he assumed the command, and beat such a skillful retreat that he brought them out of the country in safety.

The following year, when again chosen Bœotarch, Epaminondas made plans for a second campaign, and marched into Thessaly to deliver his friend, who was still a prisoner.

When Alexander the tyrant heard that Epaminondas was at the head of the army, he was frightened, and tried to disarm the wrath of the Thebans by setting Pelopidas free, and sending him to meet the advancing army.

Of course, Epaminondas was very glad to see his friend; but when he heard how cruelly Alexander treated all his subjects, he nevertheless continued his march northward, hoping to rid the country of such a bad ruler.

Just then the Spartans, in spite of their solemn promise, suddenly rose up in arms against the Thebans; and Epaminondas, leaving part of the army in Thessaly with Pelopidas, hurried southward with the rest to put down the revolt.

Pelopidas marched boldly northward, met the Thessalians, and fought a fierce battle. When it was over, theThebans, although victorious, were very sad; for their leader, Pelopidas, had been slain in the midst of the fray.

Still, undaunted by his death, the army pursued the Thessalians, and killed Alexander. Then, to show their scorn for such a vile wretch, they dragged his body through the mud, and finally flung it out of a palace window into the courtyard, where it was torn to pieces by his own bloodhounds.

LXXX. THE BATTLE OF MANTINEA.

When Epaminondas heard that his friend Pelopidas was dead, he grieved sorely; but nevertheless, knowing that his country had need of him, he vigorously continued his preparations to meet and conquer the Spartan army.

The battle promised to be hard fought; for while Epaminondas, the victor of Leuctra, led the Thebans, Agesilaus, the hero of countless battles, was again at the head of the Spartan army. The Thebans pressed forward so eagerly, however, that the two armies met at Man-ti-ne´a, in the central part of the Peloponnesus.

In spite of Agesilaus' courage and experience, and the well-known discipline of the Spartan troops, the Thebans again won a splendid victory over their foes. Their joy, however, was turned to mourning when they heard that Epaminondas had been mortally wounded just as the battle was drawing to an end.

A spear had pierced his breast; and as he sank to the ground, some of his followers caught him, bore him away tenderly in their arms, and carefully laid him down under a tree on a neighboring hillside. As soon as he opened his eyes, he eagerly asked how the army was getting along.

Gently raising him so that he could see the battlefield, his friends pointed out the Spartan army in full flight, and the Thebans masters of the field. Epaminondas sank back with a sigh of relief, but soon roused himself again to ask whether his shield were safe.

It was only when he had seen it that he would allow the doctors to examine his wound. They found the head of a barbed spear sunk deep into his breast, and said that it must be pulled out. Still they hesitated to draw it out, for they feared that the rush of blood would kill him.

Epaminondas, therefore, bade them leave it alone, although he was suffering greatly; and then he called for his assistant generals, to give them a few important orders. The friends standing around him sadly told him that both had fallen in the battle, and could no longer execute his commands. When Epaminondas heard this unwelcome news, he realized that there was no one left who could replace him, and maintain the Theban supremacy: so he advised his fellow-countrymen to seize the favorable opportunity to make peace with the Spartans.

When he had thus done all in his power to provide for the future welfare of his native city, Epaminondas drew out the spear from his wound with his own hand, for he saw that his friends were afraid to touch it.

As the doctors had foreseen, there was a great rush of blood, and they soon saw that Epaminondas had onlya few minutes to live. His friends wept over him, and one of them openly expressed his regret that Epaminondas left no children.

These words were heard by the dying hero, who opened his eyes once more, and gently said, "Leuctra and Mantinea are daughters enough to keep my name alive!"

This saying has proved true; for these two great victories are put down in every Greek history, and are never spoken of except in connection with the noble general who won them in behalf of his country, and died on the field when the last victory was secured.

In memory of Epaminondas, their greatest citizen and general, the Thebans erected a monument on the battlefield, and engraved his name upon it, with an image of the dragon from whose teeth his ancestors had sprung.

The Thebans, remembering his dying wish, then proposed a peace, which was gladly accepted by all the Greek states, for they were exhausted by the almost constant warfare they had kept up during many years.

LXXXI. THE TYRANT OF SYRACUSE.

You have seen what a cruel man Alexander was. He was not the only tyrant in those days, however; for the city of Syracuse in Sicily, which Alcibiades had hoped to conquer, was ruled by a man as harsh and mean as Alexander.

This tyrant, whose name was Di-o-nys'ius, had seized the power by force, and kept his authority by exercising the greatest severity. He was always surrounded by guards, who at a mere sign from him were ready to put any one to death.

Dionysius was therefore feared and hated by the people whom he governed, but who would have been very glad to get rid of him. No honest man cared to come near such a bloodthirsty wretch, and there were soon none but wicked men to be found in his court.

These men, hoping to win his favor and get rich gifts, used to flatter him constantly. They never told him the truth, but only praised him, and made believe to admire all he said and did.

Of course, even though they were wicked too, they could not really admire him, but secretly hated and despised him. Their praise, therefore, was as false as they, and their advice was always as bad as bad could be.

Now, Dionysius was as conceited as he was cruel, and fancied that there was nothing he could not do. Among other things, he thought he could write beautiful poetry. Whenever he wrote a poem, therefore, he read it aloud to all his courtiers, who went into raptures over it, although they made great fun of it behind his back.

Dionysius was highly flattered by their praise, but thought he would like to have it confirmed by the philosopher Phi-lox´e-nus, the most learned man of Syracuse.

He therefore sent for Philoxenus, and bade him give his candid opinion of the verse. Now, Philoxenus was far too noble a man to tell a lie: and whenever he was consulted by Dionysius, he always boldly told the truth, whether it was agreeable or not.

When the tyrant asked his opinion about the poems, therefore, he unhesitatingly answered that they were trash, and did not deserve the name of poetry at all.

This answer so angered Dionysius, and so sorely wounded his vanity, that he called his guards, and bade them put the philosopher into a prison hewn out of the living rock, and hence known as "The Quarries."

Here Philoxenus was a prisoner for many a day, although his only fault was having told the tyrant an unwelcome truth when asked to speak.

The philosopher's friends were indignant on hearing that he was in prison, and signed a petition asking Dionysius to set him free. The tyrant read the petition, and promised to grant their request on condition that the philosopher would sup with him.

Dionysius' table was well decked, as usual, and at dessert he again read aloud some new verses which he had composed. All the courtiers went into ecstasies over them, but Philoxenus did not say a word.

Dionysius, however, fancied that his long imprisonment had broken his spirit, and that he would not now dare refuse to give a few words of praise: so he pointedly asked Philoxenus what he thought of the poem. Instead of answering, the philosopher gravely turned toward the guards, and in a firm voice cried aloud, "Take me back to The Quarries!" thus showing very plainly that he preferred suffering to telling an untruth.

The courtiers were aghast at his rashness, and fully expected that the tyrant would take him at his word andput him in prison, if nothing worse; but Dionysius was struck by the moral courage which made Philoxenus tell the truth at the risk of his life, and he bade him go home in peace.

LXXXII. STORY OF DAMON AND PYTHIAS.

There lived in those days in Syracuse two young men called Da´mon and Pyth´i-as. They were very good friends, and loved each other so dearly that they were hardly ever seen apart.

Now, it happened that Pythias in some way roused the anger of the tyrant, who put him in prison, and condemned him to die in a few days. When Damon heard of it, he was in despair, and vainly tried to obtain his friend's pardon and release.

The mother of Pythias was very old, and lived far away from Syracuse with her daughter. When the young man heard that he was to die, he was tormented by the thought of leaving the women alone. In an interview with his friend Damon, Pythias regretfully said that he would die easier had he only been able to bid his mother good-by and find a protector for his sister.

Damon, anxious to gratify his friend's last wish, went into the presence of the tyrant, and proposed to take the place of Pythias in prison, and even on the cross, if need be, provided the latter were allowed to visit his relatives once more.

Dionysius had heard of the young men's touching friendship, and hated them both merely because they were good; yet he allowed them to change places, warning them both, however, that, if Pythias were not back in time, Damon would have to die in his stead.

At first Pythias refused to allow his friend to take his place in prison, but finally he consented, promising to be back in a few days to release him. So Pythias hastened home, found a husband for his sister, and saw her safely married. Then, after providing for his mother and bidding her farewell, he set out to return to Syracuse.

The young man was traveling alone and on foot. He soon fell into the hands of thieves, who bound him fast to a tree; and it was only after hours of desperate struggling that he managed to wrench himself free once more, and sped along his way.

He was running as hard as he could to make up for lost time, when he came to the edge of a stream. He had crossed it easily a few days before; but a sudden spring freshet had changed it into a raging torrent, which no one else would have ventured to enter.

In spite of the danger, Pythias plunged into the water, and, nerved by the fear that his friend would die in his stead, he fought the waves so successfully that he reached the other side safe but almost exhausted.

Regardless of his pains, Pythias pressed anxiously onward, although his road now lay across a plain, where the hot rays of the sun and the burning sands greatly increased his fatigue and faintness, and almost made him die of thirst. Still he sped onward as fast as his trembling limbs could carry him; for the sun wassinking fast, and he knew that his friend would die if he were not in Syracuse by sunset.

Dionysius, in the mean while, had been amusing himself by taunting Damon, constantly telling him that he was a fool to have risked his life for a friend, however dear. To anger him, he also insisted that Pythias was only too glad to escape death, and would be very careful not to return in time.

Damon, who knew the goodness and affection of his friend, received these remarks with the scorn they deserved, and repeated again and again that he knew Pythias would never break his word, but would be back in time, unless hindered in some unforeseen way.

The last hour came. The guards led Damon to the place of crucifixion, where he again asserted his faith in his friend, adding, however, that he sincerely hoped Pythias would come too late, so that he might die in his stead.

Just as the guards were about to nail Damon to the cross, Pythias dashed up, pale, bloodstained, and disheveled, and flung his arms around his friend's neck with a sob of relief. For the first time Damon now turned pale, and began to shed tears of bitter regret.

In a few hurried, panting words, Pythias explained the cause of his delay, and, loosing his friend's bonds with his own hands, bade the guards bind him instead.

Dionysius, who had come to see the execution, was so touched by this true friendship, that for once he forgot his cruelty, and let both young men go free, saying that he would not have believed such devotion possible had he not seen it with his own eyes.

This friendship, which wrung tears from the grim executioners, and touched the tyrant's heart, has become proverbial. When men are devoted friends, they are often compared to Damon and Pythias, whose story has been a favorite with poets and playwrights.

LXXXIII. THE SWORD OF DAMOCLES.

Dionysius, tyrant of Syracuse, was not happy, in spite of all his wealth and power. He was especially haunted by the constant fear that some one would murder him, for he had been so cruel that he had made many bitter enemies.

We are told that he was so afraid, that he never went out unless surrounded by guards, sword in hand, and never walked into any room until his servants had examined every nook and corner, and made sure that no murderer was hiding there.

The tyrant even carried his caution so far, that no one was allowed to come into his presence until thoroughly searched, so as to make sure that the visitor had no weapon hidden about his person. When his barber once jokingly said that the tyrant's life was daily at his mercy, Dionysius would no longer allow the man to shave him.

Instead of the barber, Dionysius made his wife and daughter do this service for him, until, growing afraid of them also, he either did it himself or let his beard grow.

Suspicious people are never happy; and, as Dionysius thought that everybody had as evil thoughts as himself, he was always expecting others to rob or murder or injure him in some way.

His sleep, even, was haunted by fear; and, lest some one should take him unawares, he slept in a bed surrounded by a deep trench. There was a drawbridge leading to the bed, which he always drew up himself on his own side, so that no one could get at him to murder him in his sleep.

Among the courtiers who daily visited Dionysius there was one called Dam′o-cles. He was a great flatterer, and was never weary of telling the tyrant how lucky and powerful and rich he was, and how enviable was his lot.

Dionysius finally grew tired of hearing his flattery; and when he once added, "If I were only obeyed as well as you, I should be the happiest of men," the tyrant offered to take him at his word.

By his order, Damocles was dressed in the richest garments, laid on the softest couch before the richest meal, and the servants were told to obey his every wish. This pleased Damocles greatly. He laughed and sang, ate and drank, and was enjoying himself most thoroughly.

By chance he idly gazed up at the ceiling, and saw a naked sword hanging by a single hair directly over his head. He grew pale with terror, the laughter died on his lips, and, as soon as he could move, he sprang from the couch, where he had been in such danger of being killed at any minute by the falling sword.

Dionysius with pretended surprise urged him to go back to his seat; but Damocles refused to do so, and pointed to the sword with a trembling hand. Then the tyrant told him that a person always haunted by fear can never be truly happy,—an explanation which Damocles readily understood.

Since then, whenever a seemingly happy and prosperous person is threatened by a hidden danger, it has been usual to compare him to Damocles, and to say that a sword is hanging over his head.

LXXXIV. DION AND DIONYSIUS.

When Dionysius the tyrant died at last, he was succeeded by his son, a lazy, good-for-nothing young man, who was always changing his mind. Every day he had some new fancy, admired something new, or rode some new hobby. As the son's name was the same as the father's, the latter is now sometimes known as Dionysius the Elder, while the son is generally called Dionysius the Younger.

The new tyrant had a brother-in-law named Di′on, a good and studious man, who had received an excellent education. Like most rich young Greeks of his day, Dion had gone to Athens to finish his studies; and there he had been a pupil of Plato, the disciple of Socrates.

As Dion was modest, truthful, and eager to learn, he soon became a favorite of Plato, who took great interest in him, and spared no pains to make him a fine scholar and philosopher.

When Dion came back to Syracuse, he often spoke with great warmth of his teacher. This so excited the curiosity of Dionysius, the new tyrant, that he longed to see Plato himself. He therefore begged Dion to invite Plato to Syracuse to teach him also.

The young man was very glad to do so. He hoped, that, under the philosopher's wise teachings, Dionysius would learn to be good and industrious, and thus become a blessing instead of a curse to his people. But Plato was already an old man, and answered that he could not undertake so long a journey at his advanced age.

Dion then wrote again such imploring letters, that the philosopher finally decided to change his mind, and set sail for Syracuse. There he was received at the shore by Dionysius in person, and escorted to the palace.

For a short time the tyrant listened with great pleasure to the philosopher's teachings. Then, growing weary of virtue as of everything else, he suddenly began to reproach Dion for bringing such a tiresome person to court.

All the courtiers had pretended to listen to Plato's teaching with the greatest interest; but they liked feasting better than philosophy, and now began to make fun of the great Athenian, and to turn him into ridicule.

They were so afraid that the virtuous Dion would again win their fickle master's ear, and induce him to do something really useful and reasonable, that they made up their minds to get rid of him.

By artful slander they soon made Dionysius believe that his brother-in-law was a traitor, and that his only wish was to take the power, and become tyrant of Syracuse in his stead.

Now, these accusations were not true; but Dionysius believed them, and sent Dion into exile, forbidding his wife, who loved him dearly, to go with him, and even forcing her to take another husband instead.

The courtiers wished to revenge themselves for the weary hours they had spent listening to Plato's beautiful talk, which they were too base to understand, so they now said that he had helped Dion; and they had him first put into prison, and then sold into slavery.

Happily, there were some of the philosopher's friends in town; and they, hearing of this outrage, knew no rest until they had bought his freedom, and sent him back to Athens to end his life in peace.

On his way home, Plato stopped at Olympia to attend the games. As soon as the people found out that he was there, they shouted for joy; and one and all voted him a crown just like those won by the victors in the games.

This was the highest honor the Greeks could bestow; and, although it was nothing but a wreath of olive leaves, you may be sure that the philosopher prized it more highly than if it had been of pure gold, because it was a token of the love and respect of his countrymen.

LXXXV. CIVIL WAR IN SYRACUSE.

When Dion was exiled from Syracuse by Dionysius, he went to Greece, where he was unhappy only because he could not see the wife and child he loved so dearly.

When he heard that the tyrant had forced his wife to belong to another husband, he vowed he would punish Dionysius for this crime. Plato vainly tried to persuade Dion not to return to Syracuse. The young man refused to listen to his advice, and, gathering together a small army, he set sail without delay.

He landed boldly, although he was an exile, and was welcomed with great joy by all the people, who were very weary of their ruler. When he told them that he had come to punish the tyrant, they all joined him, and marched with him up to the palace.

As Dionysius was out of town at the time, they had no trouble whatever in getting into the royal dwelling. This was hastily deserted by the tyrant's few friends, who took refuge in the citadel.

Some time after, when Dionysius came back to the city, he found the harbor blocked by a great chain stretched across it to prevent the entrance of any ship; and he was forced to retreat into the citadel, where the angry Syr-a-cus´ans came to besiege him.

Now, Dion had a great many friends, and, as everybody knew that he was truthful and well-meaning, the people all fought on his side. He was so strict with himself, however, that he treated his subjects also with great rigor, and exacted such obedience and virtue that they soon grew weary of his reign.

Then, too, while he was always ready to reward the good, Dion punished the wicked with such severity that he soon made many enemies. One of these was the courtier Her-a-cli´des, who, instead of showing his dislike openly, began to plot against him in secret.

Dionysius, besieged in the citadel, was in sore straits by this time, and almost dying of hunger; for the Syracusans, afraid that he would escape, had built a wall all around the citadel, and watched it night and day, to prevent any one from going in or out, or smuggling in any food.

As Dionysius had no army, and could not win back his throne by force, he made up his mind to do so, if possible, by a trick. He therefore wrote a letter, in which he offered Dion the tyranny in exchange for his freedom. This message was worded so cleverly that it sounded as if Dion had asked to be made tyrant of Syracuse.

LXXXVI. DEATH OF DION.

Now, after suffering so much under Dionysius and his father, the Syracusans had learned to hate the very name of tyrant; and ever since Dion had come into the city, and taken the lead, they had loudly said they would never stand such a ruler again.

As soon as the letter was ended, Dionysius tied it to a stone, and threw it over the wall. Of course, it was carried to Dion, who read it aloud, little suspecting its contents, or the effect it would produce upon his followers.

The people began to frown and look angry, and Heraclides boldly seized this opportunity to poison their minds against Dion. He urged them to drive their new leader out of the city, and to give the command of the army to him instead.

The people, ever ready for a change, gladly listened to this advice, and, after banishing Dion, made Heraclides their chief. Dionysius cleverly managed to escape from the citadel; and his general, Nyp′sius, only then becoming aware of the revolution, took his place there, and by a sudden sally won back the greater part of the city.

As Heraclides was taken by surprise at this move, and greatly feared the wrath of Dionysius, he now wrote to Dion, begging him to come back and save those who had upheld him.

The appeal was not made in vain. Dion generously forgave the treachery of Heraclides, and, marching into the city once more, drove Nypsius back into the citadel, where this general died.

The people of Syracuse were ashamed of having so suddenly turned against Dion after their first warm welcome to him, and they now fell at his feet, begging his pardon, which he freely granted to them all.

In spite of this kindness, which they had not deserved, Heraclides and many others went on plotting secretly against Dion, until his friends, weary of such double dealing, put Heraclides to death.

Dion was sorry for this, reproved his friends for committing such a crime, and said that he knew the Syracusans would in time lay the murder at his door, and try to punish him for it.

He was right in thinking thus, for the friends of Heraclides soon began plotting against him; and, entering hiscountry house one day when he was alone, they fell upon him and killed him.

As soon as Dionysius heard that Dion was dead, he hastened back to Syracuse, where he ruled more cruelly than ever, and put so many people to death that the citizens rose up against him once more. With the help of a Co-rin′thi-an army, they then freed their city, and sent Dionysius to Corinth, where he was forced to earn his living by teaching school.

The people all hooted.

As Dionysius was a cross and unkind teacher, the children would neither love nor obey him; and whenever he passed down the street, clad in a rough mantle instead of a jewel-covered robe, the people all hooted, and made great fun of him.

LXXXVII. PHILIP OF MACEDON.

In the days when Thebes was the strongest city in Greece, and when Epaminondas was the leader in his native country, he received in his house a young Mac-e-do´-ni-an prince called Philip. This young man had been sent to Greece as a hostage, and was brought up under the eye of Epaminondas. The Theban hero got the best teachers for Philip, who was thus trained with great care, and became not only quite learned, but also brave and strong.

Mac´e-don, Philip's country, was north of Greece, and its rulers spoke Greek and were of Greek descent; but, as the people of Macedon were not of the same race, the Greeks did not like them, and never allowed them to send any one to the Amphictyonic Council.

Two years after the battle of Mantinea, when Philip was eighteen years old, he suddenly learned that the king, his brother, was dead, and had left an infant to take his place. Philip knew that a child could not govern: so he escaped from Thebes, where he was not very closely watched, and made his way to Macedon.

Arriving there, he offered to rule in his little nephew's stead. The people were very glad indeed to accept his services; and when they found that the child was only half-witted, they formally offered the crown of Macedon to Philip.

Now, although Macedon was a very small country, Philip no sooner became king than he made up his mind to place it at the head of all the Greek states, and make it the foremost kingdom of the world.

This was a very ambitious plan; and in order to carry it out, Philip knew that he would need a good army. He therefore began to train his men, and, remembering how successful Epaminondas had been, he taught them to fight as the Thebans had fought at Leuctra and Mantinea.

Then, instead of drawing up his soldiers in one long line of battle, he formed them into a solid body,—an arrangement which soon became known as the Macedonian phalanx.

Each soldier in the phalanx had a large shield, and carried a spear. As soon as the signal for battle was given, the men locked their shields together so as to form a wall, and stood in ranks one behind the other.

The first row of soldiers had short spears, and the fourth and last rows very long ones. The weapons of the other rows were of medium length, so that they all stuck out beyond the first soldiers, and formed a bristling array of points which no one dared meet.

Philip not only trained his army so as to have well-drilled soldiers ready, but also found and began to work some gold mines in his kingdom. As they yielded much precious metal, he soon became one of the richest men of his time.

This wealth proved very useful, for it helped him to hire a great force of soldiers, and also to buy up a number of allies. In fact, Philip soon found that his gold was even more useful than his army, and he was in the habit of saying that "a fortress can always be taken if only a mule laden with gold can be got inside."

Philip was so kind and just that he soon won the love of all his subjects. It is said that he listened to the complaints of the poor and humble with as much patience as to those of his noblest courtiers.

Once, after dining heavily and drinking too much, Philip was suddenly called upon to try the case of a poor widow. As the king's head was not very clear, he was not able to judge as well as usual: so he soon said that she was in the wrong, and should be punished.

The woman, who knew that she was right, was very angry; and, as the guards were dragging her away, she daringly cried, "I appeal!"

"Appeal?" asked Philip, in a mocking tone, "and to whom?"

"I appeal from Philip drunk to Philip sober!" replied the woman.

These words made such an impression upon Philip, that he said he would try the case again on the next day, when his head was quite clear. He did not forget his promise on the morrow; and when he found that the woman was right, he punished her accuser, and set her free.

LXXXVIII. PHILIP BEGINS HIS CONQUESTS.

As we have already seen, when Philip found himself in the wrong, he was not afraid to admit his mistake, and to try to do better. He was also very patient and forgiving. On one occasion he heard that a man named Ni-ca´nor was always speaking ill of him.

He therefore sent for the man, who came in fear and trembling, thinking that the king would either imprison or slay him. Philip, however, received him kindly, made him sit at his own table, and let him go only after giving him many rich gifts. As the king had not found fault with him in any way, Nicanor was greatly surprised, and vowed that he would not speak another word against so generous a man.

As soon as Philip had made sure of his authority at home, drilled his army, and piled up enough gold, he began to carry out his bold plans. First of all, he wished to subdue a few of his most unruly neighbors, such as the Thracians and O-lyn´thi-ans.

An archer named As´ter came to him just before he began this war. This man offered his help to the king, and began to boast how well he could shoot. Philip, who believed only in spears for fighting, sent the man away, after saying that he would call for his help when he began to war against starlings and other birds.

This answer made Aster so angry that he went over to the enemy and enlisted in their ranks. Philip soon came to besiege the city where Aster was stationed; and as soon as the archer heard of it, he got an arrow upon which he wrote, "To Philip's left eye."

Aster then went up on the wall, took careful aim, and actually put out the king's left eye. Philip was so angry when he heard of the writing on the arrow, that he ordered another shot into the city. On this arrow was written, "If Philip takes the city, he will hang Aster."

The city was taken, and the archer hung; for Philip always prided himself upon keeping promises of this kind. The Olynthians, finding that they would not be able to resist long, now wrote a letter to the Athenians, begging them to come to their rescue.

The Athenians read the letter in the public square, so that every one could hear it, and then began to discuss whether they should send any help. As was always the case, some were for, and others against, the plan, and there was much talking. Among the best speakers of the city was the orator De-mos´the-nes, a very clear-sighted man, who suspected Philip's designs. He therefore warmly advised the Athenians to do all they could to oppose the Macedonian king, so as to prevent his ever getting a foothold in Greece. Indeed, he spoke so eloquently and severely against Philip, and told the people so plainly that the king was already plotting to harm them, that violent speeches directed against any one have ever since been called "Philippics," like these orations against the King of Macedon.

LXXXIX. THE ORATOR DEMOSTHENES.

As you have seen in the last chapter, Philip had one great enemy in Greece, the orator Demosthenes. He had distrusted Philip from the very first, and had kept warning the Athenians that the King of Macedon was very ambitious, and would soon try to become master of all Greece. When the Olynthians asked for aid, he had warmly urged the Athenians to give it, saying that they ought to bring on the conflict with Philip as soon as possible, so that the fighting might be done outside of Greece. In spite of his good arguments, however, Demosthenes failed.

Philip took not only O-lyn´thus, but all the towns which formed the Olynthian union, and destroyed them so completely that a few years later one could not even find out where these once prosperous cities had been.

Demosthenes made three very fine speeches in favor of the Olynthians, and several against Philip. These were written down, and have been translated time and again. You may some day read and admire them for yourselves.

Of course, when Philip heard of Demosthenes' speeches, he was very angry; but he thought that his gold could do wonders, so he sent a beautiful cup of that precious metal to the orator. The gift was accepted; still Demosthenes, instead of remaining silent as Philip had expected, went on talking against him as openly as before.

Demosthenes.

As Demosthenes was such a great man, you will like to hear how he learned to speak so well. He was an orphan, but very ambitious indeed. He saw how eagerly the Athenians listened to the best speakers, and he thought that he too would like to become an orator.

Unfortunately, he could not talk very plainly, and instead of listening to him, even his playmates made fun of him. But instead of crying, sulking, or getting angry, Demosthenes sensibly made up his mind to learn how to speak so well that they could no longer laugh at him. He therefore learned a great deal of poetry, which he recited daily as distinctly as possible. To be able to do this without attracting any attention, he used to go down to a lonely spot on the seashore, where he would put some pebbles in his mouth, and then try to recite so loud that his voice could be heard above the noise of the waves.

To make his lungs strong, he used to walk and run up hill, reciting as he went; and, in order to form a pleasant style, he copied nine times the works of the great Greek historian Thu-cyd´i-des.

When a young man, he shut himself up in the house to study hard. Then, as he was afraid of being tempted to go out and amuse himself, he shaved one side of his head, and let the hair grow long on the other.

You see, he was bound to succeed, and his constant trying was duly rewarded, as it always is. He became learned, eloquent, and energetic; and whenever he rose to speak in the public places of Athens, he was surrounded by an admiring crowd, who listened open-mouthed to all he said.

The Athenians were too lazy at this time, however, to bestir themselves very much, even for their own good. So, in spite of all that Demosthenes could say, they did not offer any great resistance to Philip, who little by little became a very powerful king.

XC. PHILIP MASTERS GREECE.

When Philip had entirely subdued the Thracians and Olynthians, he helped the Thessalians to get rid of their tyrant; and, adding their cavalry to his infantry, he boasted of as fine an army as the Greeks had ever been able to muster. He was very anxious to find a pretext to march into Greece at the head of this force, because he thought that, once there, he would soon manage to become master of all the towns. And the excuse for which he longed so much soon came.

A contest known as the Sacred War was going on in Greece at that time. It had arisen because the Pho´cians had taken possession of lands that were left waste in honor of the god Apollo. The Amphictyonic Council said they should pay a fine for this offense; and the Phocians, angry at being thus publicly reproved, defied the council.

To show how little they intended to obey, they not only kept the land they had taken, but robbed the temple at Delphi. Then they used the money thus obtained to win over some allies, and soon began to make war against the people who obeyed the council.

The loyal Greeks fought against the Phocians for a long time, but were unable to conquer them: so Philip proposed to come and help the council. In their anxiety to win in this war, the Greeks gladly allowed him to bring his army into their country, and he soon completely subdued the rebels.

In reward for his help, Philip was made president of the council,—a position he had long coveted, —and leader of the Pyth´i-an games held in honor of Apollo.

When the war was ended, Philip quietly went back to Macedon. He was, however, merely waiting for a favorable opportunity to reënter Greece, and punish the Athenians for listening to Demosthenes' speeches against him.

In the mean while, Philip's gold had been very busy, and he was buying up as many friends and allies as he could. Many of his gifts had the desired effect, and were not like the gold cup which he sent to Demosthenes. This, you know, had wholly failed in its purpose, for the orator went on talking more eloquently than ever against the Macedonian king.

He finally roused the Athenians to the point of arming to meet Philip, when they heard that he was really coming at last to make himself master of Greece. Their allies, the Thebans, joined them; and the two armies met at Chær-o-ne´a, in Bœotia, where a terrible battle was fought.

Demosthenes had joined the army; but as he was no soldier, and was not very brave, he fled at the very first onset. Dashing through the bushes, he was suddenly stopped by some spiky branches that caught in his cloak and held him fast. The orator was so frightened that he thought the enemy had captured him, and, falling upon his knees, he began to beg that his life might be spared.

While Demosthenes was thus flying madly, his friends and fellow-citizens were bravely meeting the Macedonians; but, in spite of all their courage, they were soon forced to yield to the Macedonian phalanx, and the battlefield was left strewn with their dead.

Alexander, Philip's son, who was then only eighteen years of age, commanded one wing of his father's army, and had the glory of completely crushing the Sacred Battalion of the Thebans, which had never before been beaten.

This brilliant victory at Chæronea made Philip really master of all Greece; but he generously refrained from making the Athenians recognize him openly as their lord, although he made their government do whatever he pleased.

As Greece was now obedient to him, the ambitious Philip began to plan the conquest of Asia and the downfall of the Persian Empire. To get as large an army as possible, he invited all the Greeks to join him, artfully reminding them of all they had suffered at the hands of the Persians in the past.

His preparations were nearly finished, and he was on the point of starting for Asia, when he was murdered by Pausanias, one of his subjects, whom he had treated very unkindly.

XCI. BIRTH OF ALEXANDER.

When Philip died, he was succeeded by his son Alexander, a young man of twenty, who had already earned a good name by leading part of the army at the battle of Chæronea. His efforts, as you know, had defeated the Sacred Battalion of the Thebans, and helped much to secure the victory.

Through his mother, O-lym´pi-as, Alexander was a descendant of Achilles, the well-known hero of the Trojan War. He was born at Pel´la, a city of Macedon, three hundred and fifty-six years before Christ. His father was so pleased to have a son, that he said that all the boys born in his kingdom on the same day should be brought up with Alexander in the palace, and become his bodyguard.

Thus you see the young prince had plenty of playmates; and, as there was nothing he liked better than fighting, he soon began to play soldiers, and to train his little regiment.

From the very first, the Macedonians had declared that Alexander was born to greatness, and several noted events that took place on the day of his birth served to confirm this belief.

In the first place, Par-me´ni-o, Philip's general, won a grand victory on that day; then Philip's horses, which had been sent to Olympia, got the prize at the chariot races; and, lastly, the famous temple at Ephesus, dedicated to Diana, was burned to the ground.

The first two events were joyful in the extreme; but the burning of this temple, which was among the wonders of the world, was a great calamity. Every one was anxious to know how it had happened; and all were very angry when they found out that it was not an accident, but had been done on purpose.

The man who had set fire to it was crazy. His name was E-ros´tra-tus; and when he was asked why he had done such a wicked thing, he said that it was only to make his name immortal. The people were so indignant, that they not only condemned him to die, but forbade all mention of his name, hoping that it would be forgotten.

In spite of this care, Erostratus' name has come down to us. It is immortal indeed, but who except a crazy man would wish to win such fame, and could bear to think that all who ever heard of him would condemn his action, and consider him as wicked as he was insane?

Alexander was first given over to the care of a nurse. He loved her dearly as long as he lived, and her son Cly´tus was always one of his best friends and most faithful comrades.

As soon as he was old enough, Alexander began to learn the Iliad and Odyssey by heart; and he loved to hear about the principal heroes, and especially about his own ancestor, Achilles.

He admired these poems so much that he carried a copy of them with him wherever he went, and always slept with it under his pillow. Both the Iliad and the Odyssey were kept in a box of the finest gold, because Alexander thought nothing was too good for them.

XCII. THE STEED BUCEPHALUS.

When only thirteen years of age, Alexander once saw some horsedealers bringing a beautiful steed before the king. The animal had a white spot on his nose shaped somewhat like the head of an ox, and on this account was named Bu-ceph´a-lus, which means "ox-head."

Philip admired the horse greatly, and bade the grooms try him, to see if his gait was good. One after another mounted, only to be thrown a few minutes later by the fiery, restless steed, which was becoming very much excited.

The horse seemed so skittish that Philip finally told the men to lead him away, adding that a man would be foolish to purchase such a useless animal. Alexander then stepped forward and begged permission to try him.

His father first made fun of him for asking to mount a horse which none of the grooms could manage; but, as Alexander persisted in his wish, he was finally allowed to make the attempt.

The young prince then quietly walked up to the excited horse, took the bridle, held it firmly, and began to speak gently and pat the steed's arched neck. After a moment, Alexander led Bucephalus forward a few steps, and then turned him around, for he had noticed that the horse was frightened by his shadow.

Then, when the shadow lay where he could not see it, and where it could no longer frighten him, the young man dropped his cloak quietly, and vaulted upon the horse's back. Once more Bucephalus reared, pranced, kicked, and ran; but Alexander sat firmly on his back, spoke to him gently, and, making no effort to hold him in, let him speed across the plain.

Alexander and Bucephalus.

In a few moments the horse's wildness was over, and Alexander could ride back to his proud father, sitting upon a steed which obeyed his slightest touch.

Philip was so delighted with the coolness, courage, and good horsemanship that Alexander had shown on this occasion, that he made him a present of the steed. Bucephalus became Alexander's favorite mount, and, while he would allow no one else to ride him, he obeyed his master perfectly.

Although most young men began the study of philosophy only at sixteen, Alexander was placed under the tuition of Ar´is-totle soon after his first ride on Bucephalus. This philosopher was a pupil of Plato. He was so learned and well known, that Philip, in writing to him to tell him of Alexander's birth, expressed his pleasure that the gods had allowed his son to live in the same age with so great a teacher.

Alexander loved Aristotle dearly, and willingly learned all that was required of him. He often said that he was very grateful, for this philosopher had taught him all the good he knew. Alexander's remarkable coolness, judgment, and perseverance were largely owing to his teacher, and, had he always followed Aristotle's advice, he would have been truly great.

But although Alexander did not always practice the virtues which Aristotle had tried to teach him, he never forgot his old tutor. He gave him large sums of money, so that the philosopher could continue his studies, and find out new things; and during his journeys he always sent him complete collections of the animals and plants of the regions he visited.

XCIII. ALEXANDER AS KING.

Philip, King of Macedon, as we have seen, had one great fault. He drank; and often his reason was clouded, and his step unsteady. Now, it is impossible to respect a man who is drunk, and everybody used to make fun of Philip when he was in that state.

Even Alexander, his own son, felt great contempt for him when he thus disgraced himself; and once when he saw his father stagger and fall after one of his orgies, he scornfully exclaimed, "See! here is a man who is getting ready to cross from Europe to Asia, and yet he cannot step safely from one couch to another."

Alexander, we are told, was greatly displeased by his father's conquests, and once angrily cried that if Philip really beat the Persians, and took possession of Asia, there would be nothing left for him to do.

You may readily imagine, therefore, that he was not very sorry when his father died before the expedition could be undertaken; for he thus became, at twenty, master of an immense army and of great riches, and head of all the Greek cities, which were then the finest in the world.

The news of Philip's death was received with great joy by the Athenians also, who thought they would now be free. Demosthenes, in particular, was so glad to be rid of his hated foe, that he ran all through the city with a crown of flowers on his head, shaking hands with everybody he met, and shouting his congratulations.

His joy was so great, because he and all his fellow-citizens fancied that a mere boy like Alexander would never be able to hold his own, and because they hoped to become again the leading people of Greece.

The Thracians, who also thought that Alexander would not be able to carry out his father's plans, now revolted, and the young king was obliged to begin his reign by marching against them.

Three months passed. The Greeks heard no news of Alexander or of his army, and fancied that he had been defeated and killed. The Thebans, thinking the right moment had come, suddenly rose up, and said that they would never again submit to the Macedonian yoke, but would stay free.

They soon had cause to repent of this rash talk. Alexander was not dead, but had conquered the Thracians completely. Without stopping to rest, he now marched straight down into Bœotia, and besieged and took Thebes. All the inhabitants were either slain or sold into slavery, the walls torn down, and not a single building was left standing, except the house of Pin´dar, a Greek poet, whose songs Alexander had always admired.

The other Greek cities, frightened by the terrible punishment of Thebes, sent messengers to the young king, offering not only to obey him as their chief, but also to supply all the men, money, and stores he wished for the expedition to Asia. Alexander graciously accepted all these proposals, and then marched southward as far as Corinth.

XCIV. ALEXANDER AND DIOGENES.

Everybody bowed down before Alexander, and all looked at him with awe and respect, as he made his triumphant progress through Greece,—all except the sage Di-og´e-nes.

This man belonged to a class of philosophers who were called "cynics," which means "doglike," because, as some say, they did not care for the usual comforts of life.

It is said that Diogenes, the principal philosopher of this kind, chose as his home a great earthenware tub near the Temple of Ce´res. He wore a rough woolen cloak, summer and winter, as his only garment, and ate all his food raw. His only utensil was a wooden bowl, out of which he drank.

One day, however, he saw a child drinking out of its hollow palm. Diogenes immediately threw away the bowl, saying he could do without luxury as well as the child; and he drank henceforth from his hand.

As you see, Diogenes was a very strange man. He prided himself upon always telling the truth, and upon treating all men alike. Some of his disciples once met him wandering about the streets with a lantern, anxiously peering into every nook and corner, and staring fixedly at every person he met. When asked what he was looking for so carefully, yet apparently with so little hope, he bluntly answered, "An honest man."

Alexander had heard of this queer philosopher, and was anxious to see him. He therefore went to the Temple of Ceres, escorted by all his courtiers, on purpose to visit him. Diogenes was lying on the ground in front of his tub, warming himself in the rays of the sun.

Alexander, drawing near, stood between the philosopher and the sun, and tried to begin a conversation; but Diogenes gave surly answers, and seemed to pay little heed to his visitor.

At last the young king proudly remarked, "I am Alexander the king!"

"And I," replied the philosopher in exactly the same tone, "am Diogenes the cynic!"

As he could win nothing but short or rude answers, Alexander was about to go away, but he first asked the sage if there was anything he could do for him. "Yes," snapped Diogenes; "stand out of my sunshine!"

The courtiers were shocked at this insolent behavior, and began to talk of the philosopher in a scornful tone as they were moving away. Alexander, overhearing them, soon stopped them by saying, "If I were not Alexander, I should like to be Diogenes."

By this remark he wished them to understand, that, if he could not be master of all earthly things, he would rather despise them.

Strange to relate, Alexander the king, and Diogenes the cynic, died on the same night, and from the same cause. Diogenes died in his tub, after a too plentiful supper from the raw leg of an ox; while Alexander breathed his last in a Bab-y-lo´ni-an palace, after having eaten and drunk to excess at a rich banquet.

XCV. ALEXANDER'S BRILLIANT BEGINNING.

As soon as the Greek states had all been brought to a proper state of obedience, Alexander prepared to conquer Persia, although he had a force of only 34,500 men. These men were very well trained, however, and promised to be more powerful on the battlefield than the million warriors of Xerxes.

In his joy at departing, Alexander made rich presents to everybody, until one of his advisers modestly reminded him that his treasure was not boundless, and asked him what he would have left when he had given away all he owned.

"My hopes!" answered Alexander proudly, for he expected to conquer not only Persia and Asia Minor, but all the known world.

While his army slowly made its way along the coast and across the Hellespont, Alexander, attended by only a few followers, sailed straight for Troy, the ancient Asiatic city.

He landed on the desert plain where the proud city had once stood, visited all the scenes of the mighty conflict, and offered sacrifices on the tomb of Achilles, while his friend He-phæs´ti-on did the same on that of Patroclus.

When this pious pilgrimage to the tomb of his ancestor was over, Alexander hastened to join the army, for he longed to do like the ancient Greeks, and win a glorious victory.

His wishes were soon granted, for before long he met the Persian army near the Gra-ni'cus River, where a terrible battle was fought. Alexander himself joined in the fighting, and would certainly have been killed had not his friend Clytus, the son of his old nurse, rushed to his rescue and saved his life.

In spite of the size of the Persian army, which was much larger than his own, Alexander won a complete victory at the Granicus. Then, marching southward, he took the cities of Sardis and Ephesus without striking another blow. These towns were very rich, and offered of their own free will to pay him the same tribute that they had given to the Persians.

Alexander, however, would not take it, but bade them use the money to rebuild the Temple of Diana, which had been burned to the ground on the night he was born. As the sacred image of the goddess had been saved, the E-phe'sians gladly built a second magnificent shrine, which was visited many years later by Paul, the disciple of Christ.

From Sardis and Ephesus, Alexander marched on into the province of Ca'ri-a. Here the queen of the country warmly welcomed him, adopted him as her son, and even proposed to give him her best cooks, so that they might prepare his food for him on the march.

Alexander thanked her heartily for this kind offer, but declined it, saying that his tutor Aristotle had given him the very best recipe for making him relish his meals.

The queen, whose appetite was fanciful, eagerly asked what it was; and Alexander smilingly answered, "A march before daybreak as the sauce for my dinner, and a light dinner as the sauce for my supper."

This was, as you may see, a very good recipe; and if Alexander had always remembered to be temperate, as Aristotle had advised, he would not have died of over eating and drinking at the age of thirty-three.

XCVI. THE GORDIAN KNOT.

Alexander did not stop long in Caria. Marching onward, he soon came to the city of Gor'di-um, in Phryg'i-a, where Mi'das had once reigned. In one of the temples the people proudly showed Alexander the cart in which this king rode as he entered their city.

The yoke was fastened to the pole by a rope tied in a peculiar and very intricate knot. Now, it seems that an ancient prophecy had declared that whoever untied the Gordian knot would surely be master of all Asia.

Of course, as Alexander had set his heart upon conquering the whole world, he looked at this knot with great interest; but a few moments' careful examination made him feel sure that he would not be able to untie it.

Rather than give it up, however, Alexander drew his sword, and cut it with a single quick stroke. Ever since then, when a person has settled a difficulty by bold or violent means instead of patiently solving it, the custom has been to say that he has "cut the Gordian knot," in memory of this feat of Alexander's.

Alexander cutting the Gordian Knot.

From Gordium, Alexander next passed on to Tar´sus, which also became subject to him; and shortly after that the young conqueror nearly lost his life.

He had been exposed to the hot sun, and had thus become terribly overheated, when he came to the river Cyd´nus. This stream was a torrent whose waters were very cold, but, in spite of all that his attendants could say, Alexander insisted upon taking a bath in it.

The sudden chill brought on a cramp, and he would have been drowned had not some of his people plunged into the water, and pulled him out. As it was, his imprudence brought on a serious illness, and for a short time Alexander's life was in great danger.

His physician, however, was Philip, a Greek doctor, who had attended him ever since he was born, and who now took great care of him. When the fever was at its worst, he said he hoped to save the king by means of a strong medicine which he was going to prepare.

Just after Philip went out to brew this potion, Alexander received a letter which warned him to beware of his physician, as the man had been bribed by the Persian king, Darius III., to poison him.

After reading the letter, Alexander slipped it under his pillow, and calmly waited for the return of his doctor. When Philip brought the cup containing the promised remedy, Alexander took it in one hand, and gave him the letter with the other. Then, while Philip was reading it, he drank every drop of the medicine.

When the physician saw the accusation, he turned deadly pale, and looked up at his master, who smilingly handed back the empty cup. Alexander's great trust in his doctor was fully justified; for the medicine cured him, and he was soon able to go on with his conquests.

XCVII. ALEXANDER'S ROYAL CAPTIVES.

Alexander was marching southward, and Darius was hastening northward with a vast army, hoping to meet him and to prevent his advancing any farther.

By a singular chance it happened that the two armies missed each other, and passed through separate defiles in the same range of mountains. Alexander became aware of this first, and retraced his steps without delay, for he was anxious to find and defeat the enemy.

The two armies soon met at a place called Is'sus, where the Persians were routed. Darius was forced to flee, and his mother, wife, and family were made captives.

As soon as the battle was over, Alexander went to visit the royal ladies in their tent, to assure them that they would be treated with all respect. He was accompanied by his friend Hephæstion, who was somewhat taller and larger than he.

As they entered the tent, in their plain armor, the queen mother, Sis-y-gam'bis, mistook Hephæstion for the king, and fell down upon her knees before him, begging his mercy for herself and her children. When she found out her mistake, she was greatly dismayed; but Alexander kindly reassured her by leaning upon his friend's shoulder, and saying of him, "He is my other self."

The young conqueror treated the Persian ladies with the utmost kindness, and often visited them in their own tent, to talk for a while with them. As he always found them idle, he fancied that time must hang very heavily upon their hands, and once offered to have them taught to spin and weave, as the Greek ladies were wont to do.

At this proposal, Sisygambis burst into tears, and asked if he wished to make slaves of them, for Persian ladies considered any labor a disgrace. Alexander, seeing her grief, hastened to comfort her, and tried to explain how happy the Greek ladies always seemed over their dainty work.

But when he understood that the royal family would rather remain idle, he never again proposed to furnish them with occupation of any kind. On the contrary, he was so gentle and respectful, that Sisygambis soon learned to love him, and used to treat him like her own son.

XCVIII. ALEXANDER AT JERUSALEM.

Darius, as we have seen, had fled after the disastrous battle of Issus. His terror was so great that he never stopped in his flight until he had reached the other side of the river Ti´gris, where he still believed himself safe.

Instead of going after Darius at once, Alexander first went southward along the coast; for he thought it would be wiser to take all the cities near the sea before he went farther inland, so as to make sure that he had no enemies behind his back.

Marching down through Syr´i-a and Phœ-nic´ia, Alexander took the cities of Da-mas´cus and Si´don, and came at last to Tyre, a prosperous commercial city built on an island at a short distance from the shore.

The Tyr´i-ans would not open their gates and surrender, so Alexander prepared to besiege the city. As he had no fleet, he began to build a great causeway out to the island.

This was a very difficult piece of work, because the water was deep; and while his men were building it, they were greatly annoyed by showers of arrows, stones, and spears from the walls of the city and from the decks of the Tyrian vessels.

A storm, also, broke the causeway to pieces once, when it was nearly finished, and the army had to begin the work anew. The obstinate resistance of Tyre made Alexander so angry, that he celebrated his final victory by crucifying a large number of the richest citizens.

After offering up a sacrifice to Hercules on the flaming ruins of Tyre, Alexander went on toward Je-ru´sa-lem. His plan was to punish the Jews, because they had helped his enemies, and had supplied the Tyrians with food.

The news of his coming filled the hearts of the Jews with terror, for they expected to be treated with the same frightful cruelty as the Tyrians. In their fear they knew not whether to surrender or fight.

Finally Jad-du´a, the high priest, had a vision, in which an angel of the Lord appeared to him, and told him what to do. In obedience to this divine command, he made the Le´vites put on their festal garments, and then, dressed in his priestly robes, he led them down the hill to meet the advancing conqueror.

When Alexander saw the beautiful procession, headed by such a dignified old man, he quickly got down from his horse, knelt before Jaddua, and worshiped the name written on his holy vestments.

His officers, astonished at this unusual humility, finally asked him why he did such honor to a foreign priest. Then Alexander told them of a vision he had had before leaving Macedon. In it he had beheld Jaddua, who bade him come over to Asia without fear, as it was written that the Persians would be delivered into his hands.

Walking beside the aged Jaddua, Alexander entered the holy city of Jerusalem and the courts of the temple. Here he offered up a sacrifice to the Lord, and saw the Books of Daniel and Zech-a-ri´ah, in which his coming and conquests were all foretold.

XCIX. THE AFRICAN DESERT.

After staying a few days in Jerusalem, Alexander continued on his way to Egypt, which he quickly conquered also. Here he founded a new city at the mouth of the Nile, and named it Al-ex-an´dri-a, after himself. It was so favorably located, that it soon became an important town, and has continued so even till the present day.

Then, having heard that there was a famous temple in Lib´y-a, dedicated to Jupiter, Alexander resolved to go there and visit it. The road lay through an African desert, and the journey was very dangerous indeed.

The soldiers toiled painfully along over the burning sand, in which their feet sank up to the ankles. The blazing African sun fell straight down upon their heads, and made them stagger and grow faint with the heat.

From time to time a hot wind, the simoom, blew over the desert, raising great clouds of dust, and choking men and horses as it rolled over them like a torrent, burying them under its shifting waves.

The horses died from thirst and fatigue, for such animals are not fit for travel in the desert. The only creature which can journey comfortably over the dreary waste of the Sa-ha´ra is the camel, whose stomach is made in a peculiar way, so that it can drink a large quantity of water at a time, and store it up for future use.

Undaunted by fatigue or danger, Alexander pressed onward. Like his soldiers, he suffered from heat and thirst; and like them, too, he was deceived by the mirage.

This is an optical effect due to a peculiar condition of the desert atmosphere. The traveler suddenly sees trees, grass, and running water, apparently a short distance before him. He hastens eagerly forward to lie in the shade, and to plunge his hot face and hands in the refreshing stream; but when he reaches the spot where he saw water and trees, there is nothing but sand, and he sinks down exhausted and cruelly disappointed.

After enduring all these hardships, Alexander arrived at last at the oasis, or green island in the sandy desert, where the Temple of Jupiter stood. The priests led him into the holy place, and, hoping to flatter him, called him the son of Jupiter.

After resting for some time in this pleasant spot, Alexander and his men again braved the dangers of the desert, went back to Alexandria and Tyre, and from there began the long-delayed pursuit of Darius.

The Greek soldiers had suffered so many hardships since beginning the war, that they were now ready for anything. They crossed the Eu-phra´tes over a hastily built bridge; then coming to the Tigris, where neither bridge nor boats could be found, they boldly swam across the river, holding their shields over their heads to protect themselves from the arrows of the Persians who stood on the other bank.

Alexander was always the first to rush forward in battle, and he now led the way across the river. He was longing to meet the Persians again, and was very glad to overtake them on the other side of the Tigris.

Here, on the plains of Ar-be´la, the third great battle was fought, and Alexander won the victory. Darius fled once more before the conqueror, while Alexander marched straight on to Bab´y-lon, the most wonderful city in the East.

C. DEATH OF DARIUS.

Alexander soon won the good will of the Babylonians by allowing them to rebuild the Temple of Bel, which had been destroyed. He also secured the affections of the captive Jews; for he excused them from doing any work on this building as soon as he heard that they considered it the Tower of Babel, and hence objected to aiding in its erection.

The young conqueror spent one month in Babylon, and then went on to Su´sa. There he found the brazen statue of Athene which Xerxes had carried off to Persia; and he sent it back to the Athenians, who received it with much joy.

The Persian queen now became very ill, and, in spite of the utmost care, she soon died. Throughout her illness, Alexander was most thoughtful and attentive; and when she died, he gave orders that she should be buried with all the pomp due to her high rank.

He also comforted the mourning Sisygambis, and sent the news of the queen's death to Darius, who had fled to the northern part of his kingdom, where he was hastily gathering together another army. Touched by Alexander's conduct, Darius now wrote to him, offering peace, and proposing to share the throne of Persia with him.

The young conqueror's head had been turned by his many victories, and he was growing more haughty every day: so he proudly refused this proposal, saying that the world could not have two masters any more than two suns.

In his pride, Alexander now assumed the dress and state of an Oriental king, surrounded himself with luxury, and spent most of his time in feasting and revelry. His courtiers encouraged him in this folly, and he soon forgot the wise lessons taught by Aristotle.

On several occasions the young king drank so much that he did not know what he was doing; and once, in a fit of drunken rage, he set fire to the beautiful palace of Per-sep´o-lis, and burned it to the ground.

As he had refused Darius' offers of peace, he soon considered it necessary to continue the war: so, laying aside his jeweled robes, he put on his armor and set out for the north. He was about to overtake the Persian king, when Darius was mortally wounded by one of his followers named Bes ´sus.

The traitor thought that he would win Alexander's favor by this crime, and came and boasted of it to him. Alexander was so angry, however, that he bade his guards seize Bessus, and had him put to death in the most barbarous way.

When the Macedonian king finally came up with Darius, he found him bathed in his own blood, and breathing his last. He had only time to assure him of the safety of his family, and to promise to continue to protect them, before Darius sank back dead.

By Alexander's orders the body was embalmed, and carried to Sisygambis, so that it could be properly buried in the beautiful tomb of the Persian kings. This last act of generosity quite won the aged queen's heart; and she felt so grateful, that she loved Alexander as long as he lived.

CI. DEFEAT OF PORUS.

Now that Darius was dead, Alexander took the Persian title of "Shah in Shah" (king of kings), and became ruler of all the empire which had been subject to the Persian monarch.

He was so proud of his new state and of his vast conquests, that he entirely forgot that he owed them mostly to his brave generals and soldiers; and he became so obstinate, that he would no longer listen to any advice, and only thought of having his own way.

His father's general, Parmenio, who had always given him the wisest counsel, was no longer in favor, because he tried to restrain the king's extravagance. Indeed, Alexander's once generous and noble nature was so changed, that, when his courtiers accused Parmenio of treachery, he listened to them, and actually put the faithful general to death.

Every day now Alexander indulged in feasts and banquets, always drinking more and more, although it was affecting his health as well as his temper. Clytus, the son of his old nurse, tried to check his excesses, but only succeeded in provoking his wrath.

On one occasion such remonstrances so enraged Alexander, that in his drunken fury he seized a spear and killed Clytus. When he saw him dead at his feet, the king realized what a terrible crime he had committed, and felt deep remorse for a short time.

He reformed, and, instead of giving himself up entirely to pleasure, spent the next two years in the work of governing Persia, where he founded several cities called by his name.

As all the central part of Asia now acknowledged his rule, he next went down into India, where he found King Po'rus, the bravest adversary he had ever met. This king, whose realm was in the northwestern part of India, came against Alexander with a very large army. In the ranks were many elephants, trained to crush the enemy beneath their huge feet, and bearing on their broad backs wooden turrets filled with brave fighting men and good archers.

In spite of these elephants, which at first awakened great fear in the Greek soldiers, the Macedonian phalanx won the victory as usual, and Porus was made prisoner. He was led into the presence of Alexander, who haughtily asked him how he expected to be treated. "Like a king!" was the proud reply.

This answer so pleased Alexander, that he not only set Porus free, but even allowed him to keep his kingdom, after he had sworn to be the faithful subject of his conqueror.

Alexander, having thus won the help and affection of Porus, made war against several other Indian kings, and continued his advance toward the south. In one of these battles he lost his faithful steed Bucephalus, which had borne him safely through many a fight.

Alexander felt this loss deeply, and not only had a monument built over his remains, but also founded a city near by, which was called Bu-ceph'a-la.

CII. THE RETURN TO BABYLON.

Upon reaching the Hyph'a-sis River, Alexander would have liked to cross it, and continue his conquests; but his soldiers now refused to go any farther. They were tired of fighting and danger, and were longing to go back to Macedon.

Although he was unwilling to do so, Alexander was therefore obliged to stop in his conquests; but, instead of going home as he had come, he now built a fleet, and sailed down the In'dus River to the sea.

Now, the Greeks had no maps such as we have; and their knowledge of geography was very small. When Alexander came to the sea, however, he thought it must be the same as that into which the Euphrates flowed.

To find out if this was true, he bade his admiral, Ne-ar'chus, sail along the coast and explore it, while the army went homeward on foot. Alexander himself staid with the army, and led the soldiers along a new way, which was very wearisome and dangerous.

The Macedonians had to pass through large wastes of burning sand, where they suffered a great deal. They were cheered and encouraged, however, by the example of Alexander, who nobly shared their hardships, and always went ahead of them on foot, carrying his own armor.

Once, when they were panting with thirst, some of his men found a little water, which they brought him. Rather than indulge in anything which all could not share with him, Alexander poured the water out uponthe sand, saying he would refresh himself only when his men could do so too.

After many months of weary travel and great suffering, the army finally joined the fleet at the mouth of the Euphrates, for Nearchus had in the mean while sailed all along the northern coast of the Indian Ocean and up the Persian Gulf.

He wrote an account of this wonderful sea journey, which was of great importance, as it opened a new and convenient road for Eastern commerce. The people soon took advantage of it to establish colonies and trading stations, and to carry on a lively business with the East.

CIII. DEATH OF ALEXANDER THE GREAT.

Alexander now went back to Babylon, where he married Rox-an´a, a Persian princess, giving her sister's hand to his intimate friend Hephæstion. This wedding was celebrated with great pomp, for eighty Macedonian officers took Persian wives on the same day.

The feasting for the weddings went on for many days, and the revelry was carried to such a shameful excess, that Hephæstion actually drank himself to death.

In token of sorrow, Alexander built him a fine tomb, had him buried with all the magnificence possible, and even decreed that he should henceforth be worshiped as a god. In this folly he was upheld by the priests, who were now ready to grant his every wish, and were always filling his mind with their senseless flatteries.

Alexander then fell into his old habits more than ever. He had again assumed all the pomp of an Eastern king, and sat on a wonderful golden throne. Over his head was the golden vine that had formerly belonged to the first Darius. Its leaves were of emeralds, while its grapes were clusters of fine carbuncles.

This vine had been given to a Persian king by Crœ´sus, the wealthy ruler of Lyd´i-a, and was considered one of the most precious treasures which the young conqueror had won.

But in spite of all Alexander's successes, he was not nearly so happy as he used to be when only king of Macedon. He no longer enjoyed the fine health which had helped him to bear the greatest hardships, and, weakened by over eating and drinking, he soon fell dangerously ill.

The doctors crowded around his bed, doing their best to save him, but they soon saw that he would die. When the Macedonian soldiers heard this, they were beside themselves with grief, and one and all insisted upon seeing their beloved leader once more.

Silently and sadly they filed past his bed, gazing upon the dying face which they had seen so bright and full of life a short time before. As most of the soldiers were older than their king, they had never expected to outlive him; and every one said that it was sad to die thus, at thirty-three, when master of nearly all the known world.

Just before he died, some one begged Alexander to name his successor. He hesitated for a moment, then drew his signet ring from his finger, gave it to Per-dic´cas, his principal general, and whispered that the strongest among them should have the throne.

Death of Alexander.

Alexander's death was mourned by all, for, in spite of his folly and excesses, he was generally beloved. Even Sisygambis, the Persian queen whom he had taken captive a few years before, shed many tears over his remains, and declared she had lost a protector who had always treated her as kindly as if he had been her own son.

The conqueror's body was laid in a golden coffin, and carried in state to Alexandria, the city he had founded at the mouth of the Nile. Here a fine tomb was built by order of Ptol´e-my, one of Alexander's generals, who said that his dead master also should be worshiped as a god.

Ptolemy wanted the body to remain in Egypt because an oracle had said that he who buried Alexander would be master of his kingdom.

CIV. THE DIVISION OF THE REALM.

The day after Alexander's death there was a sad assembly in the palace. All the Macedonian generals sat there in silence and dismay, gazing at the empty golden throne, upon which Perdiccas had solemnly laid the royal signet ring.

Who was to take the place of the king whose military genius and great conquests had won for him the title of "Great"? It is true that Alexander had a half-brother, named Ar-ri-dæ´us, but he was weak-minded. The only other heir was an infant son, born shortly after his father's death.

The generals gravely talked the matter over, and finally said that Arridæus and the child should be publicly named successors of the dead king, while four of their own number should be appointed guardians of the princes, and regents of the vast realm.

This decision was considered wise, and the kingdom of Alexander was divided into thirty-three provinces, each governed by a Macedonian officer, who was to hold it in the name of Arridæus and of the child.

In dying, Alexander had foretold that his funeral would be followed by bloodshed, and this prediction came true. The generals who had met so solemnly around the empty throne soon became dissatisfied at being only governors, and each wanted to be king in his own right, of the land intrusted to his care.

Perdiccas, having received Alexander's signet ring from his dying hand, was, of course, their leader, and took under his own protection the infant king and the Persian mother Roxana.

He fancied that it would thus be an easy matter to keep the power in his own hands, and to govern the vast realm as he pleased. But An-tip´a-ter, governor of Macedon, no sooner heard that Alexander was dead, than he placed the idiot Arridæus on the throne, proclaimed him king, and began to rule as if he were the only regent.

The other Macedonian generals daily claimed new rights, which Perdiccas was forced to grant in order to pacify them; but when it was too late, he found out how mistaken he had been, and regretted that he had yielded to their demands.

The various governors, never satisfied with the honors given them, were not only suspicious of each other, but particularly jealous of Perdiccas, the head of the realm. In their envy, they rose up against him; and for many years Perdiccas was forced to hold his own against them all, while trying to make his way back to Macedon, where he wanted to place Alexander's son upon the throne.

CV. DEATH OF DEMOSTHENES.

When Alexander left for the East, the orator Demosthenes began to urge the Greeks to rise up against him, and win back their freedom. All his eloquence, however, was not enough to persuade them to make war as long as Alexander lived.

But when the conqueror's death was made known, Demosthenes again tried to arouse them, and this time with success. Pho´cion, a cautious Athenian, vainly begged the people to wait at least until the news was confirmed, saying, "If Alexander is dead to-day, he will still be dead to-morrow and on the next day, so that we may take counsel at our leisure."

This wise caution, however, did not suit the Athenians, who were joined in their revolt by most of the little states and principal towns of Greece, except Sparta. The united Greeks soon raised an army, which marched northward, and met the Macedonian governor's troops near Thermopylæ.

The Greeks were successful here, and, after shutting up the enemy in the fortress of La´mi-a, closely besieged them. But after a time the Greek general was killed; and, when the Macedonians were reënforced, they gained a decisive victory. This really ended the war; for the Macedonian general, Antipater, broke up the union, and made separate terms of peace for each city.

In his anger, Antipater said he would punish all those who had encouraged the Greeks to revolt. He soon learned that Demosthenes had been one of the principal men to advise the uprising, so he sent his soldiers to make him prisoner.

Demosthenes, warned of his danger, immediately fled, but had only time to take refuge in the Temple of Neptune. There, in spite of the holiness of the place, Antipater's guards came to get him.

Seeing that it would be useless to resist, the orator asked for a few moments' respite, that he might write a letter to his friends. The men consented; and Demosthenes, closely watched, took up his tablet and the reed with which he generally wrote.

Phocion.

The soldiers saw him trace a few lines, then stop and bite the top of his reed, as if thinking about what he would say next. But, instead of going on to write his letter, the orator soon covered his head with his cloak and staid quite still.

After a few moments' waiting, one of the men went to him, and, receiving no answer to his question, drew aside the folds of the cloak. He started back in terror, for the orator's face was very pale, and he was evidently about to die.

The men quickly carried him out of the temple, so that it should not be defiled by death, and then they found that the reed with which he wrote was hollow, and had contained a deadly drug. Demosthenes had taken the poison, thinking that death would be better than prison.

The Athenians now saw that it would have been wiser to listen to the cautious Phocion: so they set him at the head of their affairs, and promised to obey him. Although honest, Phocion was not very clever, and his caution little by little became cowardice.

In his fear of the Macedonians, he allowed them to have more and more power; and Greece a few years later was entirely under the rule of Antipater, the Macedonian governor.

CVI. THE LAST OF THE ATHENIANS.

Antipater, although master of all Greece, did not treat the people cruelly, for he was very anxious to secure friends who would help him to keep his share of Alexander's realm.

He soon heard that Perdiccas was marching homeward with the infant king, who was named, like his father, Alexander; and he knew that the general wanted to place the child on the Macedonian throne. This plan was very distasteful to Antipater. He was not at all afraid of the infant Alexander, but he knew that Perdiccas would want to be regent, and he wished that position himself.

Rather than give up his authority, Antipater decided to fight; and, as many of Alexander's generals were dissatisfied, they all rose up in arms at the same time, as we have seen.

Perdiccas was surrounded by enemies, but he faced them all bravely, and even led an army into Egypt to subdue Ptolemy, his greatest foe. To reach the enemy, the soldiers under Perdiccas were obliged to swim across the Nile. Here so many of them were eaten up by huge crocodiles, that the rest, angry with their general for leading them into such danger, fell upon him and killed him.

Almost at the same time, Antipater died, leaving his son, Cas-san´der, and his general, Pol-ys-per´chon, to quarrel over the government of Macedon. Each gathered together an army, and tried to get as many friends as possible, especially among the Greeks.

The Athenians vainly tried to remain neutral during this quarrel; but in the course of the war, Polysperchon came into their city, said that Phocion and many other great citizens were siding with Cassander, and condemned them to die by drinking poison brewed from the hemlock plant.

It seems, however, that there was not enough poison ready to kill them all, so the jailer made Phocion give him some money to buy more. The noble old man, forced to do as he was bidden, gave the necessary amount, saying, "It seems that one cannot even die for nothing in Athens."

As he was the last really noted politician in the city, he has been called the "Last of the Athenians." No one ever dared to uphold the city's power after his death, or tried to help it win back its old freedom.

As soon as Perdiccas was dead, Roxana and her son were brought to Macedon, where they were finally placed under the protection of Polysperchon. When Olympias, the mother of Alexander the Great, saw his infant son, she was so anxious to secure the throne for him alone, that she slew the idiot king Arridæus and all his family.

Under pretext of avenging this crime, Cassander captured and slew Olympias; and then, having won Macedon and Greece from Polysperchon, and seeing that there was no one left to protect Roxana and the child king, he put both mother and son in prison, where they were killed by his order shortly after.

Thus, twelve years after Alexander's death, all his family were dead, and his vast kingdom was a prey to quarreling, which broke it up into several states.

CVII. THE COLOSSUS OF RHODES.

When Perdiccas died, An-tig´o-nus ("the one-eyed") was named his successor, and became governor of all the Eastern province. He no sooner heard that Cassander had murdered Alexander's family, than he marched westward, intending to avenge the crime.

On his way, Antigonus passed through Syria, the land governed by Se-leu´cus, and asked that ruler how he had spent the money of the kingdom. Seleucus, who had a bad conscience, instead of answering, ran away to Egypt, where he became a friend of Ptolemy.

Then, fearing that they would not be able to fight against Antigonus successfully, these two generals persuaded Cassander, ruler of Macedon, and Ly-sim´a-chus, ruler of Thrace, to join them.

For several years the war was kept up between the four allies on one side, and Antigonus and his son De-me´tri-us on the other. The field of battle was principally in Asia Minor. The fighting continued until the generals became weary of warfare, and concluded to make peace.

A treaty was then signed, settling the claims of all parties, and providing that all the Greek cities should have their freedom. This done, each went back to his own province; but it soon became evident that the peace would not last, for Cassander did not keep his promise to make the Greek states free.

When Cassander's wrongdoing became known, the generals called upon Demetrius to bring him to terms. The Athenians were so pleased when they heard of this, that they received Demetrius with great joy.

Demetrius was such a good general that he soon managed to defeat Cassander at Thermopylæ; and when he came back to Athens in triumph, the happy people gave him the title of "The Preserver," called a month by his name, lodged him in the Parthenon, and worshiped him as a god. Some time after this, Demetrius conquered Ptolemy, who had shown that he would not abide by the treaty either. This victory was so great, that Demetrius' soldiers said he deserved a reward, and named him King of Syria.

When the other generals heard that Demetrius and his father had accepted the title of kings, they too put on royal crowns. Then, as each was still jealous of the rest, and wished to obtain more land for himself, war soon broke out among them once more.

Demetrius, who had been very lucky in all his wars, now planned to take the Island of Rhodes from Ptolemy, King of Egypt. It proved, however, a far more difficult thing than he had expected, and, after besieging the principal city for a whole year, he gave up the attempt.

But he had invented so many machines to try to subdue the city of Rhodes, that every one thought he deserved much credit, and they therefore gave him the title of Po-li-or-ce'tes ("the city taker").

Peace was agreed upon, and Demetrius retreated, giving up to the Rho'di-ans all the mighty war engines he had brought with him. These were sold for three hundred talents (something over three hundred thousand dollars), and the money thus obtained was used in erecting a colossal statue in honor of Apollo (or He'li-os), the patron god of the island.

Demetrius Poliorcetes. (Coin.)

This marvelous brazen statue, which was so fine that it was one of the seven wonders of the ancient world, represented the sun god, with his head surrounded by rays, and with his feet resting one on each side of the entrance of the port.

We are told that the Co-los'sus of Rhodes, as this statue was generally called, was so tall that ships under full sail easily passed under its spreading legs in and out of the harbor.

It stood there for about sixty years, when it was overthrown by an earthquake. After lying in ruins for a long time, the brass was sold as old metal. It was carried off on the backs of camels, and we are told that nine hundred of these animals were required for the work.

Thus vanished one of the much talked of wonders of the ancient world. The others were Diana's Temple at Ephesus, the Tomb of Mau-so'lus (which was so fine that any handsome tomb is sometimes called a mausoleum), the Pha'ros or Lighthouse of Alexandria or Messina, the Walls and Hanging Gardens of Babylon, the Labyrinth of Crete, and the Pyramids of Egypt. To these is often added the Parthenon at Athens, which, as you have seen, was decorated by the carvings of Phidias.

CVIII. THE BATTLE OF IPSUS.

Demetrius, having failed to take Rhodes, now passed over into Greece, hoping to overthrow Cassander; but the other kings, growing afraid of him, agreed to help the ruler of Macedon. They therefore collected a large army, and forced Demetrius to stop and fight them all at Ip'sus, in Asia Minor.

Here, just twenty years after Alexander's death, his generals met in a great battle. Seleucus, it is said, brought a number of fighting elephants, such as Porus had used, which added much to the confusion and fierceness of the struggle.

Antigonus, the father of Demetrius, was slain, and Demetrius himself was defeated, and driven to Ephesus. The Athenians, who had been his friends and allies as long as he was prosperous, now basely deserted him. They declared themselves his enemies, and made a law whereby any one who spoke well of him, or tried to make peace with him, should be put to death.

The battle of Ipsus decided the fate of Alexander's kingdom. It was now divided into four principal parts. Ptolemy remained master of Egypt, and his family reigned there many years, until under Cle-o-pa'tra, the last of his race, the country fell into the hands of the Romans.

Seleucus and his descendants, the Se-leu'ci-dæ, had the Persian Empire, or Syria and the land between the Indus and the Euphrates. The capital of this empire was first Se-leu'cia, near Babylon, and later An'ti-och, which became a rich and well-known city.

Lysimachus was given the kingdom of Thrace, which, however, soon passed into other hands; and

Cassander remained master of Macedon. As for Demetrius, although he had lost a kingdom at the battle of Ipsus, he soon managed to conquer another.

In his anger at the Athenians, he first marched against them, and besieged them in their own city. The Athenians were frightened, for they knew how well they deserved punishment; but they resisted as well as they could, and the siege dragged on for several months.

At the end of this time there was no food left in the city, and the people suffered greatly from hunger. Finally they were obliged to yield; and Demetrius rode into Athens in triumph.

CIX. DEMETRIUS AND THE ATHENIANS.

The Athenians trembled with fear when they saw the stern expression on Demetrius' face as he entered their city. This terror became still greater when he ordered all the principal citizens to assemble in the public square. None of the Athenians dared to disobey, and they were in no wise reassured when the conquering army surrounded them, each soldier holding an unsheathed sword in his hand.

Demetrius now sternly addressed the citizens, who fancied that every moment would be their last. He reproved them harshly for their ingratitude and desertion, and told them that they deserved death at his hands; but he ended his speech by saying that he preferred to show his power by granting them forgiveness rather than by killing them.

Then he went on to tell them, that, knowing how much they had suffered, he had sent supplies of grain to every house, so that when they went home they should not find their wives and children starving.

The sudden reaction from their great terror proved almost fatal to the Athenian citizens. But when they recovered their breath, the air was rent by a mighty shout of joy in honor of the kind conqueror.

Although Demetrius was as generous as he was brave, his end was very sad. After a long life of continual warfare, and after conquering and losing Macedon, he fell into the hands of his rival and enemy, Seleucus, who kept him in prison as long as he lived.

About this time a new trouble befell Macedon and Greece. This was an invasion of the Gauls, who came sweeping down from the mountains into Greece, in order to rob the temple at Delphi.

A second time, however, the temple escaped, thanks to a terrible thunderstorm, which filled the superstitious minds of the robbers with dread. In the sudden darkness the Gauls fell upon each other, as the Persians had done in the days of Xerxes, and fought so desperately that many were killed.

The Greeks, remembering former victories, now made up their minds to strike a blow in their own defense. They collected an army, and defeated the invaders so severely that Bren'nus, the leader of the Gauls, killed himself in despair, while his followers withdrew to a province in Asia Minor, which from the Gauls was called Ga-la'tia.

CX. THE ACHÆAN LEAGUE.

While the generals and successors of Alexander were busy trying to crush one another, most of the Greek towns, left to their own devices, had become small republics. But instead of forming a union, they became so jealous, that they began to quarrel and even to fight among themselves.

As the quarrels became more bitter, two parties or leagues were formed, which, from the two most important provinces at that time, received the names of Achæan and Æ-to´li-an.

The Achæan League was made up of twelve small towns in the Peloponnesus, and was under the leadership of A-ra´tus, a native of Sic´y-on. When a child, Aratus had seen his native city in the hands of a tyrant. His father, who was a patriot, had made a bold attempt to free the city, but had failed, and lost his life. Aratus, who was but seven years of age, heard that his father and all his family had been slain, and knew that the tyrant would try to kill him too. As he was too weak to defend himself, he sought refuge in the house of the tyrant's sister, where no one would be likely to seek for him.

This woman, touched by the child's trust, hid him cleverly, and, when all danger was over, sent him to some friends, where she paid for his board, and had him carefully brought up.

As Aratus was patriotic, he was anxious to finish the work which his father had begun. At the age oftwenty, therefore, he assembled a few comrades, entered Sicyon, called all the lovers of liberty to his aid, and drove away the tyrant without shedding any blood.

The town, thus freed, joined the Achæan League, of which Aratus soon became the leader. This office was elective, and no one was expected to fill it for more than a year; but Aratus was so much loved that he was chosen leader thirty-five years in succession.

At this time, Greece and Macedon were under the rule of Antigonus Go-na´tas, son of Demetrius; for this man had conquered for himself the second kingdom which his father had lost. But now Aratus and the Achæan League refused to obey him, so he marched down from Macedon to restore order.

To prevent his advance, and to hinder his getting even as much as a foothold in the peninsula, Aratus wanted to capture the fortress of Ac-ro-co-rin´thus, which barred the Isthmus of Corinth.

This undertaking was very difficult, because the fortress was perched upon a rock so high and steep that it was almost impossible to climb it.

A traitor, Di´o-cles, however, offered to show Aratus a way to climb this rock, provided that he should receive a certain reward. Although general of the Achæan League, and one of the greatest men of his day, Aratus was far from being rich; and, in order to obtain the required sum, he had to sell all he had, and even pawn his wife's few jewels.

Then, in the midst of the darkness, one rainy night, Diocles led the Achæan soldiers along a steep path, which they had to climb in Indian file.

He brought them safely and unseen into the fortress, where they killed most of the Macedonian sentinels, and put the guards to flight. As soon as the key of the Peloponnesus had been thus daringly won, most of the other towns in the peninsula joined the league, and the Achæans gained such victories, that Antigonus Gonatus fell ill, and died of grief.

The Achæan League became stronger and stronger; and, although Sparta and a few other cities remained neutral, most of the small towns were freed from their tyrants. Such was the importance of the league, that the Roman ambassadors once came to ask for its aid to suppress the pirates who infested the neighboring seas.

This help was cheerfully given, and the Achæans entered into a treaty with the Romans. They little suspected, however, that the city whose name was then almost unknown would in less than a hundred years become strong enough to subdue them, and be mistress over all Greece.

CXI. DIVISION IN SPARTA.

While the Achæan League was doing its best to restore Greece to its former power, Sparta had remained inactive. The Spartans had changed greatly since the days of Lycurgus. They no longer obeyed his wise laws, and, instead of being brave and frugal, they were greedy, lazy, and wicked.

One of their kings was named Leonidas; but he was in no way like his great namesake, the king who had fallen at Thermopylæ. Indeed, he married an Eastern wife, and to please her assumed all the pomp and led the idle life of an Eastern king.

His fellow-king, on the other hand, was such a miser that he heaped up great treasures. When he died, his wife and mother were said to have more gold than the city and people together. The miser king was succeeded by his son, but this young man's sole ambition was to restore Sparta to its former condition.

His name was A´gis. He lived like the Spartans of old, practiced all the virtues of his ancestors, and was frugal and brave in the extreme. To restore Sparta, real Spartans were needed, but, in counting them over, Agis found that there were only about seven hundred of the old stock left. The first move was to restore equality. For that purpose, all the money and land would have to be equally divided, so Agis began by persuading his own mother and grandmother to give up their wealth. Leonidas did not like the plan of equality, and soon openly opposed it, although his son-in-law Cleombrotus sided with Agis, and upheld it.

But the people were eager for the new division which would make them all equal as of old; and they were so angry with Leonidas for his resistance, that they rose up against him, and proposed to depose him by reviving an old law which forbade the ruling of a king who married a foreign wife.

Leonidas had time to flee to the Temple of Athene; and when the ephors called him to appear before them, he refused to do so, because he feared for his life. As such a refusal was a crime, the ephors said he should not reign any longer, and named Cleombrotus king in his stead.

Cleombrotus and Chilonis.

Leonidas, who had led a selfish, pleasure-loving life, was now forsaken by every one except his daughter, Chi-lo´nis, who gave up her husband and the throne in order to console her unfortunate father. She kept him company in the temple, cared for him and amused him, and, when her husband begged her to come back, she answered that her place was rather with her unhappy father than with her prosperous husband.

When it became known that the Spartans were plotting to kill the unhappy Leonidas, Agis helped him to escape, and Chilonis followed him into exile.

The Ætolian League, which just then was very strong, now sent an army across the isthmus to attack the Spartans. The latter sallied forth under the leadership of Agis, who proved such a skillful general, that he not only won a great victory, but also drove the Ætolians out of the peninsula.

During the absence of Agis, many of the richest Spartans who had not yet given up their property refused to do so, and when urged by Cleombrotus to obey, they revolted against him, and recalled Leonidas.

Cleombrotus had only time to take refuge in the same temple where his father-in-law had once found shelter. Here he was soon joined by his wife, Chilonis, who, ever faithful to the most unhappy, came thither to comfort him.

Leonidas was so angry that he would probably have treated Cleombrotus with the utmost severity, had notChilonis fallen at his feet and begged him to spare her husband's life. Her tears touched her father, and he granted the favor she asked, declaring, however, that Cleombrotus should go into exile.

In spite of her father's entreaties to remain with him, Chilonis insisted upon accompanying her husband. She gave Cleombrotus one of their two children, clasped the other to her breast, and left the city, proudly walking at her husband's side.

CXII. DEATH OF AGIS.

When Agis heard of the changes which had been taking place in Sparta during his absence, he quickly went home. On arriving in the city, he found the party of the rich so powerful that he could not oppose them, and was even forced to seek refuge in a temple, as Leonidas and Cleombrotus had each done in turn.

His wife, A-gi-a´tis, forced by illness to stay at home, could not show her love by following him there; but a few faithful friends went with him, and kept guard over him. Their watchfulness was needed, because Agis slipped out of the temple every night to go to the bath and refresh himself.

It happened, however, that two of these friends were false. They basely took the bribes offered by the ephors for information about the king, and told them that he left the temple every night, and for what purpose.

Thus advised, the ephors surprised the little party the next night, and thrust Agis into prison. He was tried and condemned to death by order of Leonidas, and thus died when only twenty-two years of age, after having vainly tried for three years to bring the Spartans back to their former simplicity and virtue.

Leonidas, not content with killing Agis, gave the widow Agiatis in marriage to his son, Cle-om´e-nes, who was a mere boy, several years younger than she. Agiatis soon won great influence over the young prince, and told him so much about her dead husband, that he tried to follow the example of Agis in everything.

When Leonidas died, Cleomenes succeeded him, and, thanks to the teachings of his wife, was both great and virtuous. He drove away the ephors, who were rich and corrupt, and then distributed all the property equally among the people, as Agis had planned.

When Aratus heard of the reforms made by Cleomenes, he began to fear that Sparta would win back her former power, and again try to lord it over the rest of Greece. To prevent such a misfortune, he decided to attack the Spartan king while he was too young to excel in the art of war.

He therefore advanced with a good army; but, to his surprise and dismay, he was completely defeated by the young king. Several of the smaller towns now showed a desire to leave the Achæan League and join Sparta, so Aratus became more eager than ever to suppress her rising power.

In his eagerness he forgot all caution, and even asked help of Antigonus Do´son, King of Macedon, the successor of Antigonus Gonatas. This ruler owed his surname of Doson ("who will give") to a bad habit of promising all kinds of gifts to his followers,—promises which were never kept.

Antigonus Doson was only too glad to send a Macedonian army into Greece, and not only garrisoned the fortress on the Isthmus of Corinth, but also sent troops on into the Peloponnesus.

CXIII. THE WAR OF THE TWO LEAGUES.

The Achæan and Macedonian armies now met the Spartans at Sel-la´sia, in Laconia, where the latter were badly defeated, and Sparta fell into the enemy's hands. Antigonus was so proud of his victory that he burst a blood vessel upon hearing the news, and died shortly after.

Before he closed his eyes, however, he had the satisfaction of driving Cleomenes away from Greece into Egypt. There the young king fell upon his sword, after killing his children, rather than become a slave. Tyrants were now allowed again in many of the Greek cities, in spite of the remonstrances of Aratus, who learned only too late that the Macedonians had come into the Peloponnesus merely for the purpose of making themselves masters of the country.

Aratus' eyes were opened. He saw that all his efforts were vain, and that, owing to his own imprudence, Greece would never again be free. In his grief, his presence of mind quite forsook him. He did not know what steps to take in order to undo all the harm he had done.

The Ætolians now became the champions of freedom, and marched against the Achæans, whom they defeated. In their distress, the Achæans once more begged the Macedonians to interfere, and send troops into Greece.

The contest which followed is known as the War of the Two Leagues, and lasted for some time. In the beginning, the Macedonian king allowed Aratus to take the lead, and followed all his directions; but, growing weary of this subordinate part, he finally poisoned the Achæan leader, and became head of the league himself.

When the Spartans and Ætolians, who had joined forces, found that the Achæans and Macedonians were likely to prove too strong for them, they also began to look around for allies. As the fame of the rising city of Rome had reached them, they finally sent thither for the help they needed.

The Romans were then rapidly extending their territory, and hoped soon to become masters of the world, so they were glad to help the Spartans against the Macedonians, who were already their enemies.

They therefore speedily came to the Spartans' aid, set fire to the Achæan and Macedonian ships, and defeated their armies so sorely, that Philip was obliged to beg for peace and to give them his son as a hostage.

The Spartans, having thus freed themselves from the yoke of the Achæan League, now fell into far worse hands, for they were governed by a tyrant named Na´bis,—a cruel and miserly man, who, in order toincrease his treasure, often had recourse to vile stratagems.

He had made a cunning instrument of torture, on purpose to obtain money from any one he wished. This was a statue, the exact image of his wife, clad in magnificent robes. Whenever he heard that any man was very rich, Nabis used to send for him. After treating him with exaggerated politeness, the tyrant would gently advise him to sacrifice his wealth for the good of the state.

If his guest refused to do so, Nabis would invite him to visit his wife, and lead the unsuspecting man close to the statue. This was made so as to move by a system of cunningly arranged springs, and as soon as the victim came within reach, the statue's arms closed tightly around him.

The terrified guest, caught in an irresistible embrace, then found himself drawn closer and closer, and pressed against sharp points and knives hidden under the rich garments.

It was only, when the tortured man had solemnly promised to give up all he owned, that the tyrant Nabis would set him free; but if he resisted, he was killed by slow torture, and allowed to bleed to death in the statue's embrace.

CXIV. THE LAST OF THE GREEKS.

When Aratus died, the principal man in the Achæan army was Phil-o-pœ´men, a brave and virtuous young man. He was patriotic in the extreme,and so plain and unassuming that no one would have suspected his rank.

On one occasion, when he had reached the dignity of general, he was invited to dine at a house where the hostess was a stranger to him. When he came to the door, she took him for a servant, on account of his plain clothes, and curtly bade him go and split wood.

Without saying a word, Philopœmen threw aside his cloak, seized an ax, and set to work. The host, on coming up a few minutes later, was horrified to see his honored guest cutting wood, and was profuse in his apologies for a mistake which only made Philopœmen laugh.

When Philopœmen heard how cruel Nabis was, he wanted to free Sparta from his tyranny. So he entered the town at the head of an armed force of men, confiscated the treasures for the benefit of the public, and drove Nabis away.

The Spartans were at first very grateful to the Achæans for freeing them, but they soon began to feel jealous of their power, and again rose up in revolt against them. This time Philopœmen treated the Spartans with the utmost severity, even razing the walls of the city, which were never rebuilt.

Philopœmen was farsighted enough to see from the beginning that the Roman alliance would prove bad for Greece. He soon discovered that the Romans intended to subdue the country, and in order to do so most easily were trying to make the people quarrel among themselves.

All his efforts were therefore directed toward keeping peace, and for a time he was quite successful. But the Romans, seeing no other way to bring about a quarrel, at last bribed the Messenians to revolt.

In the course of the war, Philopœmen was led into an artfully arranged ambuscade, and was taken in chains to Messenia, where, notwithstanding his gray hair, he was exposed to the jeers of the common people.

After thus humiliating him, they led him to the place of torture; but when he heard that his army had escaped from the ambush, he fervently cried, "I die happy, since the Achæans are safe."

This only hastened the end of the brave patriot, who has been called the "Last of the Greeks," because he was the last to try to maintain his country's independence.

The Achæans soon after took the town of Messenia, stoned all Philopœmen's murderers on his tomb, and carried his ashes to Meg-a-lop'o-lis, his native city, where they were buried with great pomp.

CXV. GREECE A ROMAN PROVINCE.

For centuries the Greeks had been in the habit of assembling at Corinth every three years for the celebration of the Isthmian games, in honor of Poseidon, god of the sea. Here, as at Olympia, there were races, wrestling and boxing matches, and contests in verse and song; and as usual the prizes were simple crowns of olive leaves, which were considered far more precious than silver or gold.

In 196 B.C. not only were the Greeks present at this celebration, but there were also many Romans who wished to witness the games. The Greeks were then particularly happy because the War of the Two Leagues seemed to be ended, and the country was at peace.

In the midst of the festival, Quin'tius Flam-i-ni'nus, the Roman consul, mounted the orator's block, and proclaimed that the Roman army had just won a great victory over the revolted King of Macedon, and that the Greek states were now indeed free.

These tidings were received with such a tumult of joyful cries, it is said, that a flock of birds that were flying overhead fell to the earth, stunned by the shock of cheers which rent the air.

This joy, however, did not last very long, for the new-won freedom of Greece existed in name only. As soon as the Romans had completed the conquest of Macedon under its last ruler, Perseus, they prepared to annex Greece also.

Their first move was to accuse the Achæans of sending aid to Macedon. Under this pretext, one thousand leading citizens were seized, and sent to Rome to be tried.

Here they were kept in exile for many a year, longing to go home, and fuming against their detention. When they were finally allowed to return, they were so imbittered, that, as the Romans had foreseen, they soon stirred up a revolt among the Achæans.

Æ-mil'i-us Pau'lus, the conqueror of Macedon, then marched into Greece, and swept over the whole country. He took the city of Corinth, and burned it to the ground, after carrying off many of its most precious works of art to adorn his triumph.

Such was the ignorance of the Romans at that time, however, about all matters of art, that the sailors who were to carry these treasures to Rome were warned by the consul to be careful, as they would have to replace any article they had damaged or lost.

The Romans then placed garrisons in the principal Greek towns, and the country became a mere province of Rome, under the name of Achaia.

Thus ends the history of ancient Greece, which, though so small, was yet the most famous country the world has ever known,—the country from which later nations learned their best lessons in art, philosophy, and literature.

CPSIA information can be obtained
at www.ICGtesting.com
Printed in the USA
LVHW111116240219
608564LV00003B/518/P